TRAVELBUG

# Tenerife

D0715426

*p*

TRAVELBUG

# Tenerife

Edited, designed and produced in 2006 by Automobile
Association Developments Limited for Parragon, Queen Street
House, 4 Queen Street, Bath BA1 1HE, UK

Published by AA Publishing (a trading name of Automobile
Association Developments Limited, whose registered office
is Fanum House, Basing View, Basingstoke, Hampshire,
RG21 4EA. Registered number 1878835).

ISBN-10: 0-7495-4649-2
ISBN-13: 978-0-7495-4649-6

Material in this book may have appeared in other AA
publications.

A CIP catalogue record for this book is available from the
British Library.

Printed and bound by Everbest, China

Find out more about AA Publishing and the wide range of
services the AA provides by visiting our website at
www.theAA.com

A02441

# contents

## KEY TO SYMBOLS

Throughout the guide a few straightforward symbols are used to denote the following categories:

| | | | |
|---|---|---|---|
| ✉ | address or location | ♿ | facilities for visitors with disabilities |
| ☎ | telephone number | 👋 | admission charge |
| 🕐 | opening times | ↔ | other places of interest nearby |
| 🍴 | restaurant or café on premises or nearby | ℹ | tourist information |
| 🚌 | nearest bus/tram route | ❓ | other practical information |
| 🚢 | nearest ferry stop | ► | indicates the page where you will find a fuller description |

This book is divided into six sections to cover the most important aspects of your visit to Tenerife.

**Essence of Tenerife** pages 10–11

**10 Top Tips** pages 12–13

**10 Top Places** pages 14–37
Our choice of the Top Ten attractions in Tenerife, with practical information.

**Discover Tenerife** pages 38–195

Four sections: The North, The South, The West and La Gomera each with brief introductions and an alphabetical listing of the main attractions

Practical information
4 suggested walks
4 suggested tours
Listings of the best places to eat and stay

**Shopping and leisure** pages 196–231

Detailed listings of the best places to eat, stay, shop, take the children and be entertained.

**What you need to know** pages 232–49

A practical section containing essential travel information.

**Maps**

A list of the maps that have been used in this travel guide can be found in the index (pages 250–253).

**Prices**

Where appropriate, an indication of the cost of an establishment is given by € signs:

€€€ denotes higher prices, €€ denotes average prices, while € denotes lower charges.

Tenerife is like two places in one. In the north it's Spanish with working towns and villages. In the south it's a basking holiday land of vibrant entertainment. While the north has an almost tropical, productive lushness, the south is rainless and dry.

For many visitors nothing can tear them away from days in the sun and nights on the town. For others it's a delight to explore the 'real' Tenerife, getting to know this beautiful volcanic land and its people. And some, of course, enjoy both sides of Tenerife.

**If you only have a short time to visit Tenerife, or would like to get a really complete picture of the island, here are the essentials:**

• **Go up Pico del Teide** The high point of Tenerife, a snow-capped dormant volcano worshipped by the Guanches, the original inhabitants of the island. From here you can see almost the whole of the Canary Islands (➤ 20).

• **Experience Playa de las Américas** Leave the real world behind and enter the package holiday dreamland, in a purpose-built town of artificial beaches, all-night discos, English pubs and restaurants that proudly boast 'No Spanish Food Served Here!' (➤ 142).

• **Go bananas** Eat Tenerife bananas, have them flambéed for dessert, drink banana liqueur, buy souvenirs made of banana leaves and visit Bananera El Guanche (➤ 96) – all because bananas are an important crop here.

• **Eat a Canarian stew** Try *potaje*, *rancho canario* or *puchero* – vegetables and meat simmered to a savoury perfection. With bread, locals consider it a complete meal.

• **Get spicy** You must try the pleasantly spicy local sauce called *mojo*. Served with fish or *papas arrugadas* (wrinkly potatoes), it's the most Canarian thing on the menu.

• **Drink a local wine** One of the first big successes for colonial Tenerife was the development of drinkable wines to rival those in mainland Spain. The island's wines have remained important ever since. La Gomera, too, has good local wines.

• **Get out of the resorts** Walk, drive or cycle, but one way or another see the Tenerife most tourists miss.

• **Watch a whale** Join one of the boat excursions to see the whales and dolphins that live just off southern Tenerife and La Gomera (► 213).

• **Have fun at a fiesta** It's an unusual fortnight in the Tenerife calendar that doesn't have at least one fiesta. Ask the tourist office what's on next.

• **Go to another island** Take the ferry to La Gomera for a truly unspoiled Canary island. If you're on La Gomera, take the boat trip over just to visit Pico del Teide.

# Casa de los Balcones, La Orotava

**The most famous sight in the sedate Spanish colonial hilltown of La Orotava is an intriguing 17th-century mansion**

When you enter the impressive front doors of Calle San Francisco you will find the exquisitely carved wooden balconies of the courtyard. Here abundant refreshing greenery, earthenware pots and an old wine press give a cool, elegant air. The building's history is told in the museum upstairs: originally it consisted of two separate houses built in 1632 as homes for prosperous colonists.

Downstairs in the busy souvenir and craft shop, a major stop-off point for coach tours, an additional attraction is local craftspeople demonstrating how to roll a cigar, weave a basket, or paint sand in readiness for the big Corpus Christi celebrations. This unusual shop sells, in addition to popular souvenirs, a wide range of high-quality items such as Spanish and Canarian lace and linen, and traditional handcrafted Canarian embroideries. Some small items – such as handkerchiefs – give an opportunity to buy good quality local goods at affordable prices.

✉ Calle San Francisco 3, La Orotava ☎ 922 330629 🕓 Mon–Fri 8.30–6.30, Sat 8.30–7.30, Sun 8.30–1.30 🍴 Restaurants and bars in Plaza de la Constitución 🚌 345 and 350 (Puerto de la Cruz–La Orotava) every 20–30 min; 348 same route once daily ✋ Museum cheap; courtyard and craft shop free

# Drago Milenario

Just how old is this amazing tree? The age of the 'Thousand-Year-Old Dragon Tree' is often exaggerated to two or even three thousand years – in reality, this majestic specimen, the oldest known, probably dates back about 600 years.

**The drago or dragon tree is a species peculiar to the Canary Islands, and this extraordinary ancient example has become an island emblem.**

More remarkable perhaps is that the species itself – *Dracaena draco*, closely related to the yucca – has barely evolved since the age of the dinosaurs. It has long been an object of fascination, not just among modern botanists, but among all who are sensitive to magic and mystery. That's partly because of its curious form, growing like a bundle of separate trunks clinging together before bursting to create the drago's distinctive mushroom shape. Weirdest of all is the drago's strange resin, which turns as red as blood on contact with the air. Though nothing is known of Guanche beliefs, many people insist that the drago was worshipped by these first inhabitants of the island, who used its resin for embalming.

Standing 17m high and with a diameter of 6m, the Drago Milenario is the main attraction at Icod de los Vinos (▶ 115), a little wine town on the west coast. The gigantic tree is protected in a garden, while bars and souvenir shops around cash in on the tree's mystique.

✉ Parque del Drago (by the church), Plaza de la Constitucíon 1, Icod de los Vinos 🤚 Free 🍴 Bars/ cafés nearby (€) 🚌 354 and 363 (Puerto de la Cruz–Icod) every 30 min ❓ Icod holds a Dragon Tree Festival in Sep

# Pico del Teide

**The highest mountain in all Spain is an active – but sleeping – volcano, soaring majestically above the Atlantic island it helped to create.**

Pico del Teide was aflame as Christopher Columbus passed this way. The sailors took it for an ill omen, Columbus for a good one. Before the Spanish conquest, the Guanche people of Tenerife – and the other islands too – revered this conical mountain crested with snow and fire. The most recent eruption was a small one in 1898, and the volcano has been quiet since; it has made some noises of late and scientists are monitoring any risk.

Over many millennia, Pico del Teide's eruptions have added more and more land to the island of Tenerife, though the terrain all around the volcano is a blasted landscape of twisted rock and debris, a devastation that thrills and amazes visitors. This region now has protected status within the Parque Nacional del Teide (➤ 122).

Pico del Teide is a mere remnant of the original Tenerife volcano, the cone of which at some point blew itself to pieces in a massive eruption. The relics of the cone surround Pico del Teide in a ring of lesser volcanic outlets, which are known as the Caldera de las Cañadas.

The 3,718m mountain does not always permit people to visit, guarding itself in mist, snow or powerful winds – sometimes even when the weather is fine down on the coast. In the height of summer, heat can be a problem, often reaching 40°C. However, on fine, calm days the summit can be approached either on foot in around 3 hours or, more usually, by *teleférico* (cable car) in 8 minutes. The cable car can, however, involve long waits (over an hour is not unusual).

Permits are required for the final 163m above the terminal, a steep scramble on loose scree (➤ 23).

A single well-worn footpath makes its way to the summit from the car park below Montaña Blanca, close to the lower cable-car terminal. Only experienced walkers, properly equipped, should attempt any other route. It is easier to walk up than down, so consider taking the cable car one way. The

path first climbs Montaña Blanca, which you may consider rewarding enough by itself. Bear in mind that altitude sickness may be a problem, so go slowly to minimise this risk.

On the final climb to the top, there's a whiff of sulphur in the air. You pass impressive smoke holes some 50m across. Take this climb gently, carry water with you, wear a sunhat and sunglasses, and carry a light sweater to wear at the summit. Whether by foot or by *teleférico*, the view is dramatic and the experience unforgettable.

✉ Parque Nacional del Teide 🍴 Nearest eating places are the *parador* and at El Portillo. The cable-car station has refreshments 🚌 348 from Puerto de la Cruz to Teide cable car once daily, leaving Puerto 9.15 and reaching cable car 11.15. Return trip 4.15. Bus 342 from Playa de las Américas to Teide cable car once daily, leaving Playa 9.15, arriving cable car 11.15. Return trip 3.40. Bus times can be unreliable ♿ None ✋ Cable car expensive; free on foot
**Cable car hotline** ☎ 922 010445, am only 🕐 Doesn't run in windy weather. Last descent 5pm ❓ Permits to climb the last 163m to peak from cable-car station are restricted to 150 per day. They are availble from the National Park office ✉ Calle Emilio Calzadilla 5, near Plaza del Príncipe, Santa Cruz 🕐 Mon–Fri 9–2 ☎ 922 290129. All applicants require passports. Check the cable car and weather before starting.

# Garachico

**For 200 years, vessels set sail laden with wine and sugar from Garachico, Tenerife's busiest port. Then in one night the harbour was destroyed.**

Created as a port by Genoese entrepreneur Cristobal de Ponte in 1496, the original Garachico became a prosperous colonial town and so it remained for two centuries. Today it lies partly buried beneath the present town – on 5 May 1706 the Volcan Negro (just south of the town) roared into life, pouring lava through Garachico and into its harbour. The islanders laid out new streets on the land formed by the lava. But the harbour (originally much larger) never recovered, and Garachico, with its fine mansions and cobbled streets, became a handsome relic.

Around the main square the old Franciscan monastery, Convento de San Francisco, pre-dates the eruption. It now houses the Casa de la Cultura, which hosts events and exhibitions and the Museo de las Ciencias Naturales, a mix of local flora, fauna and history. Don't miss the pictures showing the route of the lava flow.

Parque Puerta de Tierra, a lush sunken garden alongside Plaza de Juan González de la Torre, was part of Garachico's harbour. A huge arch which marked the port entrance has been dug out of the lava and re-erected in the square, while close by an enormous wine press also pre-dates the eruption.

For a tremendous view, go up to the roof of Castillo de San Miguel. This dark 16th-century fortress of the counts of Gomera stood firm as the lava flowed past. Today it contains a little museum and craft stall.

🍴 Isla Baja (€€) Canarian dishes; Casa Ramón (€) for local atmosphere  🚌 363 (Puerto de la Cruz–Buenavista) hourly

# Loro Parque, Puerto de la Cruz

**The premier family attraction on Tenerife is a tropical wildlife park that mixes conservation, education, entertainment and fun.**

From simple beginnings in 1972 as a parrot park (which is what Loro Parque means), this is now an award-winning zoological park, an extravaganza of tropical gardens, a dolphinarium and sea-life centre, with related attractions and rides. It's home to a colony of male gorillas for breeding, and has a water zone where the ever-popular sea lions and dolphins seem to relish their role as a holiday entertainment. The park's aquarium tunnel, believed to be the longest in the world, is a transparent underwater walkway 18.5m long. As you walk along, sharks slip through the water, just a few centimetres away. There are flamingos, crocodiles, cranes, giant turtles, jaguars, monkeys and a

Nocturnal Bat Cave. Another highlight is Planet Penguin.

Parrots, however, remain an important element of the park. There are over 300 species living here. The birds are being studied, and the park is engaged in important breeding and conservation work. While endangered parrot species may be confined, the more common varieties are used in parrot shows several times each day.

✉ 1.5km west of Plaza del Charco near Punta Brava ☎ 922 373841 ⏰ Daily 8.30–6.30 (last admission 5pm) ♿ Good ✋ Expensive 🍴 Choice on site (€–€€) 🚌 Free shuttle bus from Avenida de Colón (near Lido) and Plaza del Charco every 20 min

# Los Gigantes

One of Tenerife's most breathtaking sights is best seen from a boat: properly known as Acantilados de los Gigantes, the soaring dark rock face rising 600m from the Atlantic marks the abrupt edge of northwestern Tenerife's Teno Massif. There's nothing more to the site but its sheer grandeur, but that's enough to attract visitors. Come by car or coach and join a sightseeing boat when you arrive or take a boat excursion from one of the resorts. It's not until you see another boat cruising gently at the foot of these cliffs that their true majesty becomes clear.

**These stupendous sheer cliffs are called The Giants, an apt description of a rock face that soars 600m from blue sea to blue sky.**

The cliffs rise from one end of a pleasant bay called La Canalita. At the other end of the bay there's a small resort with a quiet, civilised feel and a black sand beach called Playa de los Guios. Being slightly remote, it preserves a calm holiday atmosphere now rare on the island. The cliffs and the sea guarantee that this little resort cannot expand much.

South of Los Gigantes, however, the coast has been heavily developed, mostly with apartments. An excellent black sand beach called Playa de la Arena near the former fishing village of Puerto de Santiago creates a focal point to the urban sprawl.

✉ 2km from Puerto de Santiago on the west coast 🛈 Edificio Seguro del Sol 36–37, Playa de la Arena ☎ 922 860348 🍴 Bars and restaurants near marina (€–€€) 🚌 325 (Puerto de la Cruz) or 473 to south coast resorts 🚢 Excursions from Puerto de Santiago, Playa de las Américas and Los Cristianos

# Mercado Nuestra Señora de África, Santa Cruz

The generosity of the Canaries and their surrounding ocean, and their ready access to all the abundance of the rest of Spain, are daily apparent in the wonderful displays in this lively and atmospheric enclosed market. Flowers fill the eye, alongside the colours of myriad fruits and vegetables, and other stalls are laden with fish and meat. You'll find small live animals, a multitude of curious peasant cheeses made of cow's, sheep's or goat's milk (or sometimes all three) and home-made honey. Here too traders sell inexpensive cassettes and CDs – often of foot-stamping Spanish and Latin American music. Interestingly, all is neat and orderly, with a surprising tidiness and efficiency.

**Tenerife's main produce market, the Market of Our Lady of Africa, is a dazzle of colour and energy, a picture of the island's abundance.**

The market is located near the heart of the old quarter of Tenerife's capital town, not far from the lanes of a red light

district, and usually spills out into these surrounding streets, where stalls sell 'dry goods' – kitchenware, fabrics and household items. The market entrance itself is a circular arch, leading straight into the flower stalls. Beyond lies a veritable bazaar within the central courtyard.

There's officially no market here on Sunday, but that's when the big weekly *rastro* sets up outside the market hall. A *rastro* is a mixed flea market and craft market, where an array of stallholders from home and abroad sell a hotch-potch of cheap souvenirs, second-rate factory-made 'craft' items, leather goods, assorted cast-offs and secondhand items, as well as plenty of genuine high-quality arts and crafts. Philatelists will love it: stamps are a particular speciality of several stallholders.

✉ Just off Calle de San Sebastián, at the south end of Puente Servador, Santa Cruz ☎ 922 606090 ⊕ Mon–Sat 8–1 (Sun *rastro* market 10–2) ♿ Few ❓ Watch out for pickpockets! Tourists at the market are seen as easy prey

# Museo de Antropología de Tenerife, Casa de Carta

**A fascinating collection of Canary Islands folk culture, housed in a fine restored country mansion, one of the most beautiful buildings on the island.**

This beautiful, low Canarian farmhouse and country mansion dates from the end of the 17th century, and is one of Tenerife's architectural gems. The building is an exquisite arrangement of carved wooden doors, balconies, porticos and patios. It stands among tropical gardens overlooking the village of Valle de Guerra.

For centuries the home of the Carta family, regional administrators, the building now houses the Tenerife Anthropology Museum. Reconstructed rooms reveal much about rural life in Tenerife, and there are examples of all the island's folk arts and crafts. Inside, 14 exhibition rooms with their galleries are used to re-create appealing little glimpses of ordinary life in the rural Tenerife of past times. The principal displays are of weaving, needlework and pottery, as well as farm tools, fabrics, clothing, ceramics and furniture.

The most interesting exhibits are of traditional Canarian dress from the 18th century onwards, highlighting the small but important differences of style and colour between one island and the next. Embroidered and patterned festival clothes, wedding clothes and everyday workwear are on show.

✉ Calle Vino 44, 38270 Valle de Guerra, La Laguna (near Tacoronte, about 25km from Puerto de la Cruz) ☎ 922 546308/922 546300
🕐 Tue–Sun 9–7. Open only during exhibitions – there are ususally exhibitions taking place 🖐 Moderate (Sun free)

# Nuestra Señora de la Concepción, La Laguna

**When Guanche leaders were 'persuaded' to become Christian and submit to Spanish rule, they were brought to this grandiose church to be baptised.**

The oldest church on the island, with much outstanding craftsmanship, Our Lady of the Immaculate Conception represents a landmark in Canarian history and has the status of a Spanish national shrine. Its greatest claim to fame is that the big glazed 16th-century baptismal font, brought here from Seville in southern Spain, was used to 'convert' defeated Guanche warriors to Christianity. You'll find it in the *baptisterio* (baptistery) set to one side of the main entrance, with family trees displayed above.

Though much changed since its foundation in 1502, even in those days the church was extraordinarily grand for a far-flung colony, with elaborately carved gilded wooden ceiling panels in Moorish design. Over the centuries, the church benefited from the finest workmanship on the island, its

Gothic origins becoming overlaid with Renaissance style and then baroque decoration.

The triple-nave church has probably the grandest and richest interior on Tenerife, and rivals any other building in the Canaries. The gold and silver paintwork and metalwork are breathtaking, together with rich retables from the 17th century and later. Immediately obvious on entering the building, the extravagant woodcarving of the 18th-century pulpit is considered one of Spain's best examples of this type of work. The choir stalls, too, are beautifully carved.

The eye-catching seven-storey tower, dating from the 17th century, has a distinctive Moorish look and is the principal landmark of this historic town.

✉ Plaza del la Concepción, La Laguna 🕐 Usually Mon–Fri 11–1, 5–8. Sat–Sun services only 🖐 Cheap 🍴 Bars/restaurants nearby 🚌 102 (Puerto de la Cruz or Santa Cruz–La Laguna) every 30 min

# Parque Nacional de Garajonay, La Gomera

**A vast area of protected forest covers the central upland of La Gomera: a strange, dark wilderness of lichens, ravines and laurel canyons.**

While sun beats down on the southern shore, a cooler, damper climate prevails around Mount Garajonay. Heather, ferns and lichens flourish, creating a thick carpet across the boulders and rocky slopes where the last of the native Canarian laurel woodland survives. Waterfalls and streams splash through the greenery. Walking in this wet, magical terrain among the slender, sinuous limbs of the Canary laurel (*Larus canariensis*), it is certainly hard to believe that you are in the Canary Islands. Not just laurel but also the luxuriant Canary date palm (*Phoenix canariensis*) grows here in great numbers, and there are around 400 species of native flowers, some found only at this place. There are also rare insects and birds.

A useful starting point is the **Centro de Visitantes (Visitor Centre)** at Juego de Bolas, on the north side of the forest. This gives an overview of the park and details all the waymarked forest walks. The centre has much else about La Gomera, including gardens, a small museum, and displays about island life over the centuries. Craftspeople demonstrate traditional skills such as weaving, pottery, basketwork and carpentry.

Easy, popular walks start at La Laguna Grande in the middle of the forest, where there's a small information centre, a woodland play area, a board showing marked trails, and a track up to a lofty *mirador* (viewpoint).

🖐 Free 🍽 Restaurants at La Laguna Grande (€€)
**Centro de Visitantes**
✉ Juego de Bolas, near Las Rosas (35km from San Sebastián)
☎ 922 800993 🕓 Tue–Sun 9.30–4.30. Craft workshops open Tue–Fri only 🚻 Few 🖐 Free

# The North

The real life of Tenerife is all in the north. Here the whole history of Tenerife can be told, for the Guanches mainly occupied the northern half, and the Spanish too settled and cultivated this area. Until package holiday holidays took off in the 1960s, even holidaymakers rarely ventured south of Puerto de la Cruz, except for the essential excursion to Pico del Teide. As a result, almost all of the island's art, culture, its Spanish colonial legacy, and its best sightseeing, are in the north.

It's the climate that is responsible for this: the north and northwest, facing the trade winds, catch all of Tenerife's gentle rain. Parts of this fertile half of the island are exotically verdant, with tropical flowers and greenery. That's what attracted the first aristocratic tourists, who adored the permanent springtime, rich crops and garden landscape of northern Tenerife.

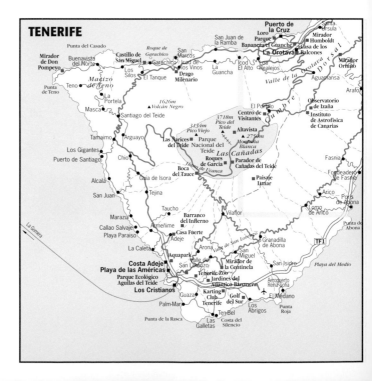

**TENERIFE**

Punta del Casado

Mirador
de Don
Pompeyo

Buenavista
del Norte

Castillo de
San Miguel

*Roque de
Garachico*

Garachico

San
Juan de
los Vinos

San Marcos

San Juan
de la Ramba

Puerto de
la Cruz

Loro Parque

Bananera el Guanche

Santa
Úrsula

Mirador
Humboldt

Casa de los
Balcones

La Orotava

Los Silos

El Tanque

Drago
Milenario

Icod

La
Guancha

El Alto

Los
Realejos

*Valle de la Orotava*

Dorsal

Aguamansa

Mirador
Ortuño

Teno

*Macizo
de Teno*

La
Portela

Masca

Santiago del Teide

*1626m
▲Volcán Negro*

El Portillo

Arafo

Observatorio
de Izaña

Instituto
de Astrofísica
de Canarias

Punta
de Teno

3134m
▲Pico Viejo

3718m
▲Pico del
Teide

Centro de
Visitantes

Altavista ▲

*Cumbre*

Tamaimo

Arguayo

Las Narices
del Teide

Parque
Nacional del
Teide

2275m ▲
Montaña
Blanca

*Las Cañadas*

Los Gigantes

Chío

Roques
de García

Parador de
Cañadas del Teide

Fasnia

Puerto de Santiago

Boca
del Tauce

*Llano de
Ucanca*

Fondeadero
de Fasnia

Alcalá

Guía de Isora

Paisaje
Lunar

Arico

Porís
de Abona

San Juan

Tejina

Vilaflor

Lomo
de Arico

Punta de
Abona

Taucho

Barranco
del Infierno

Marazul

Armeñime

Callao Salvaje

Casa Fuerte

Adeje

*Valle de San Lorenzo*

Granadilla
de Abona

San Isidro

**TF1**

*Playa del Medio*

Playa Paraíso

La Caleta

Arona

San
Miguel

Aquapark

Costa Adeje
Playa de las Américas

Valle de
San Lorenzo

Mirador
de la Centinela

Tenerife Zoo

Parque Ecológico
Aguilas del Teide

Jardines del
Atlantico Bananera

Aeropuerto
Reina Sofía

El Médano

**Los Cristianos**

Karting
Club
Tenerife

Golf
del Sur

Los
Abrigos

Punta
Roja

Guaza

Palm-Mar

Ten-Bel

Costa del
Silencio

Punta de la Rasca

Las
Galletas

La Gomera

Punta
de Teno

Punta del Hidalgo
Punta
del Hidalgo
Bajamar
Tejina
Chinamada
Taganana
Mirador
El Bailadero
Las
Carboneras
Punta de
Anaga
Valle de
Guerra
Mirador Cruz
del Carmen
Parque Rural
de Anaga
Igueste
Museo de Antropología
de Tenerife
Tegueste
Mirador Pico
del Inglés
San Andrés
Montañas de Anaga
Playa de las
Teresitas
Bosque de las
Mercedes
Mesa del Mar
Las Canteras
Guamasa
El Sauzal
Tacoronte
TF5
Nuestra Señora de la Concepción
La Laguna
Club Nautico
Aeropuerto
de Los Rodeos
La Cuesta
SANTA CRUZ
DE TENERIFE
Casa del Viño
la Baranda
La Victoria
de Acentejo
La Matanza
de Acentejo
La Esperanza
Taco
Jardín
Botánico
Santa
Úrsula
Mirador Pico
de las Flores
Bosque
de la
Esperanza
TF1
Puerto de
la Cruz
Loro
Parque
Montaña
Grande
Las
Raíces
Bananera El Guanche
Mirador
Humboldt
La Orotava
Casa de los
Balcones
Mirador de
los Cumbres
Los
Realejos
Mirador Ortuño
Valle de la Orotava
Dorsal
Aguamansa
Las Caletillas
El Portillo
Cumbre
Observatorio
de Izaña
Arafo
Candelaria
Basílica de Nuestra
Señora de Candelaria
Instituto de Astrofísica
de Canarias
Pirámides
de Güímar
Güímar
Mirador de
Don Martín
Puerto de Güímar
Gran Canaria
Fasnia
Paisaje
Lunar
Fondeadero
de Fasnia
Lomo
de Arico
Arico
Poris
de Abona

0        10        20 km

0        5        10 miles

## SANTA CRUZ DE TENERIFE

**Santa Cruz, the island's capital, still has the authentic feel and look of colonial Spain. It's not a holiday resort, but a vibrant Latin city where many Tinerfeños live and work. The name means Holy Cross of Tenerife, and comes from the crucifix planted boldly at this spot by the ruthless Spanish conqueror Alonso Fernández de Lugo, when he strode ashore in 1493 with 1,000 men to take possession of the Guanches' island home.**

During the five centuries since the conquest, Santa Cruz has remained the focal point of Tenerife's culture and history. While the gaudy, multicultural Tenerife of modern tourism stays way down south, the resolutely Spanish capital has remained almost unaffected by the millions of package-holiday visitors. Only tourists determined to know and understand the island, and looking for something more than a suntan, choose to stay here. But it's also due to the diverse economy of the capital, resulting in its oil processing, waterfront industry and deep-water harbour.

Now though, Santa Cruz has polished up some of its treasures and even provides a jaunty little 'train' to take people on a tour of the sights. At the same time, holidaymakers have realised there's more to Tenerife than *bierkellers* and crowded black beaches, and that much of the best sightseeing is in and around Santa Cruz. The redeveloped waterfront area with its diverse shipping continues to be a source of interest, while just north of the city lies a little-known treasure, the best beach on Tenerife.

**ℹ** Palacio Insular (ground floor), Plaza de España
**☎** 922 239592 **🕐** Mon–Fri 8–6, Sat 9–1

**SANTA CRUZ DE TENERIFE**

Parque Municipal García Sanabria

EL TOSCAL

Puerto

HORACIO NELSON

PLAZA 25 DE JULIO

Plaza de Toros

PLAZA DE LA PAZ

RAMBLA DEL GENERAL

RAMBLA DE PULIDO

CALLE RAMÓN Y CAJAL

Capitanía General

NUMANCIA

CALLE MÉNDEZ NÚÑEZ

CALLE DEL PILAR

AVE 25 DE JULIO

CALLE ROBAYNA

PLAZA DE WEYLER

CALLE DEL ÁNGEL GUIMERÁ

PLAZA DEL PRÍNCIPE

Círculo de Amistad XII de Enero

Museo Municipal de Bellas Artes

Iglesia de San Francisco

BETHENCT ALFONSO

CALLE DE LA ROSA

SAN FRANCISCO

AVENIDA DE FRANCISCO LA ROCHE

PLAZA DE ESPAÑA

CASTILLO

PLAZA DE LA CANDELARIA

Monumento de los Caídos

Correos

Barranco de Santos

CALLE GALCERÁN

PUENTE SERRADOR

VALENTÍN SANZ

IMELDO

SERIS

Teatro Guimerá

Centro de Fotografía

Museo de la Naturaleza y El Hombre

PLAZA DE LA IGLESIA

Palacio Insular

Iglesia de Nuestra Señora de la Concepción

CALLE DE SAN SEBASTIÁN

LA SALLE

Estadio H Rodríguez López

Parque de D Quijote

CALLE DE SAN SEBASTIÁN

Mercado de Nuestra Señora de África

JOSÉ MANUEL GUIMERÁ

AVE BRAVO MURILLO

ANTONIO PRIMO DE RIVERA

NUEVA DÁRSENA SUR

0    100    200    300 m

0    150    300 yards

JOSÉ HERNÁNDEZ ALFONSO

AVENIDA

AVENIDA TRES DE MAYO

AV TRES DE MAYO

Estación de Guaguas

AVENIDA DE LA CONSTITUCIÓN

Castillo de San Juan
Auditorio de Tenerife

## DISCOVER SANTA CRUZ

### IGLESIA DE NUESTRA SEÑORA DE LA CONCEPCIÓN (CHURCH OF OUR LADY OF THE CONCEPTION)

One of the city's most important landmarks, this church is also one of its most significant historical monuments. Begun in 1502, much changed in the 17th and 18th centuries, the church was reopened in 1999 after many years of restoration. The cross which de Lugo first placed on Tenerife soil has been kept here, as has the British flag captured from one of Nelson's ships during his 1797 raid. An additional feature of this fine church is the tomb of Nelson's opponent, General Gutierrez, defender of Santa Cruz.

✉ Plaza de la Iglesia 🕐 Daily 9–1, 5.30–8
♿ Free 🍴 Nearby in Plaza de la Candelaria (€€)

### IGLESIA DE SAN FRANCISCO (CHURCH OF ST FRANCIS)

This delightful church combines simplicity with elaborate, abundant decoration. Most striking are the wooden ceiling, a painted arch, a fine organ and two baroque *retablos* (altarpieces) dating from the 17th and 18th centuries. To the right of the high altar is a separate chapel with a Moorish-style ceiling. The church, built in 1680, was originally part of the Franciscan monastery of San Pedro de Alcántara, said to have been founded by Irish refugees fleeing from Elizabeth I's anti-Catholic rule. The monastery no longer exists, but the buildings now house the Municipal Fine Arts Museum (▶ 53); the square in which it stands was once the friary garden.

✉ Calle Villalba Hervás ⏰ Mon–Fri 9–1, 5.30–8 ♿ None 💷 Free
🍴 Café del Príncipe (€–€€) in Plaza del Príncipe

### MERCADO DE NUESTRA SEÑORA DE ÁFRICA, SANTA CRUZ (▶ 30–31)

## MUSEO MILITAR REGIONAL DE CANARIAS
## (CANARIES REGIONAL MILITARY MUSEUM)

*Todo por la Patria* – All for the Fatherland – is the inscription above the gateway into this collection of important relics from the military past of the Canary Islands. Housed in part of the 19th-century barracks, Cuartel de Almeida, the museum is proud and patriotic in tone. The oldest exhibits are the simple weapons used by the Guanches against the Spanish. Among various later insignia and memorabilia, a highlight of the collection is El Tigre, the cannon used to defend Santa Cruz against Nelson's 1797 attack and believed to be responsible for the loss of his right arm. Flags taken from one of Nelson's defeated ships, HMS *Emerald*, are also displayed. Even more compelling is the small section devoted to General Francisco Franco, dictator of Spain from 1936 to 1975. A map shows the route of the plane *Dragon Rapide*, which flew from Croydon in southern England to Tenerife, picked up the future dictator and took him to Morocco, from where he launched his coup.

✉ Calle San Isidro 2 ☎ 922 843500 🕐 Tue–Sun 10–2 ♿ Few
✋ Free ❓ Take your passport to the Muséo Militar – you probably won't be admitted without it!

walk

Start in the waterfront Plaza de España (► 58), dominated by its Civil War memorial and the massive Palacio Insular, in which the tourist office and Tenerife's council authorities (Cabildo) are housed.

*Walk into the adjoining square, Plaza de la Candelaria.*

This agreeable pedestrianised square (► 61) has good bars, craft shops and sights, including the Banco Español de Credito in the charming 18th-century Palacio de Carta.

*At the end of the square, continue on Calle del Castillo.*

This is the main shopping street of Santa Cruz, a lively, colourful avenue of little shops with gaudy signs, 'bazaars' and mingled crowds of tourists and locals.

*Continue to Plaza de Weyler.*

There's an Italian white marble fountain at the centre of this popular square. To one side stands the Capitanía General, where Franco lived while he was based here.

*At the northern tip of the square, turn along Calle Méndez Núñez.*

This less interesting street soon leads to the Parque Municipal García Sanabria (▶ 57), an enjoyable green space away from street noise where you can relax on the tiled benches.

*Take Calle del Pilar, opposite the park's south side. Follow this street to Plaza del Príncipe.*

In the slightly raised square, once the friary garden of a Franciscan monastery, luxuriant laurel trees shade a bandstand. To one side the Municipal Fine Arts Museum (▶ 53) occupies the former monastery, alongside its church, the Iglesia de San Francisco (▶ 48).

*Calle de Béthencourt leads the short distance back to Plaza de España.*

**Distance** 3km **Time** 1 hour walking, plus 2 hours sightseeing
**Start/end point** Plaza de España **Lunch** Café del Príncipe (€€)
✉ Plaza del Príncipe ☎ 922 278810

## MUSEO MUNICIPAL DE BELLAS ARTES
## (MUNICIPAL FINE ARTS MUSEUM)

It comes as a surprise, perhaps, that Tenerife's excellent Municipal Fine Arts Museum was opened in 1900, long before the tourism boom. Together with the city library, it is housed in the pleasant setting of a former Franciscan monastery. The 10 busts lined up outside are of Tenerife artists, musicians, writers and thinkers. Inside, the collection on two storeys includes the work of Canarian artists, several of historical interest, and other distinguished European works mainly covering the 17th to the 19th centuries. Most interesting are the frequent temporary exhibitions of art works loaned by Spain's leading museums of art.

✉ Calle José Murphy 12, Plaza del Príncipe ☎ 922 244358
🕐 Tue–Fri 10–8, Sat–Sun 10–2. Closed Mon ♿ Few ✋ Free
🍴 Café del Príncipe (€€) ↔ Iglesia de San Francisco (➤ 48)

## MUSEO DE LA NATURALEZA Y EL HOMBRE (MUSEUM OF NATURE & MAN)

This worthy museum, in an attractive former hospital with a galleried courtyard, deals seriously but accessibly with the archaeology, anthropology and ethnography of the Canary Islands, as well as their natural history. This is essentially two museums in one – Nature and Man are dealt with separately – and is split in half, following the plan of the building. Archaeology and the history of the Canaries lie on the left of the entrance and the fauna and flora of the islands on the right. Ten sections tackle these aspects of the Canary Islands with displays as varied as African and pre-Columbian art, aboriginal therapy, the Canaries during the Spanish Conquest and the Islands today.

✉ Calle Fuente Morales ☎ 922 535816
🕐 Tue–Sun 9–7 ♿ Good ✋ Moderate (Sun free)
🍴 Nearby in Plaza de la Candelaria

## PARQUE MARÍTIMO CÉSAR MANRIQUE
## (CÉSAR MANRIQUE MARINE PARK)

When the Cabildo (Island Council) of Tenerife wanted to do something with the unsightly disused industrial dockyards near the old Castillo de San Juan, they commissioned the brilliant Canarian artist and designer César Manrique to create something for them.

Manrique believed that tourism would be the salvation of the Canary Islands if carefully controlled, but could ruin the islands if given free rein. At Santa Cruz his brief was limited, but Manrique managed to redesign the dockland site into an attractive leisure complex linking the sea with the Castillo.

The Castillo (1641) was part of the town's defences (the Castillo San Cristóbal was located where the Plaza de España lies now). It was once a marketplace for African slaves.

Today the Parque Marítimo is a delightful lido, with palms and sunbathing terraces around a beautiful seawater pool (similar to the Lago Martiánez César Manrique created for Puerto de la Cruz, ➤ 94). To the east of the fort lies the town's new Auditorio. Designed like a sea-shell by Santiago Calatrava, it is Santa Cruz's main concert hall. Southwards stretches a huge palm park (Palmetum), still being planted, while across the busy coastal highway is a large, eye-catching exhibition space for trade fairs and conferences.

✉ Avenida de la Constitución ☎ 922 202995 🕐 Daily 10–6
🚌 909 and others along Avenida de la Constitución ♿ Good
✋ Moderate 🍴 Choice on site (€–€€€) ↔ Mercado Nuestra Señora de África (➤ 30–31)

## PARQUE MUNICIPAL GARCÍA SANABRIA

This delightful 6ha park full of shrubs, trees, exotic flowers, fountains and tranquil corners is the largest – and probably the most beautiful – urban park in the Canaries. Popular with locals, it was laid out in the 1920s and is named after the mayor of that time. He is honoured by a large monument in the centre of the park.

The somewhat incongruous pieces of modern sculpture are the product of an international street sculpture competition held in 1973. There is also a zoo, a play area and an intriguing floral clock. Take a break on the tiled benches, stroll the gravel pathways or get a snack at one of the little kiosks.

✉ Off Rambla del General Franco 🚌 Town buses along Rambla del General Franco
♿ Good (but gravel paths) ✋ Free
🍴 Snacks available at park kiosks (€)
↔ Museo Municipal de Bellas Artes
(► 53), Iglesia de San Francisco (► 48)

### PLAZA DE ESPAÑA

A large square near the waterfront, this spacious plaza is the heart of the city. The whole square was formerly the site of the principal Santa Cruz fortification, Castillo San Cristóbal, demolished in 1929. Here now stands the grimly imposing Franco-era Palacio Insular, seat of the Cabildo or Island Council, built in what was known as Rationalist style. The huge central Monumento de los Caidos, Monument to the Fallen, honours local people who fell in war, including the Spanish Civil War – Franco's manifesto was broadcast from here. The monument is flanked by statues of two *menceys* (chieftains).

✉ Off Avenida de José Antonio Primo de Rivera 🍴 Bars and cafés nearby (€–€€) 🔄 Plaza de la Candelaria (➤ 61)

## PLAZA DE LA CANDELARIA

This pleasant traffic-free square has good bars and shops, including an *artesanía* (craft shop). Centuries ago, it was the entrance to the vanished Castillo San Cristóbal, once one of the two main defences of the town (the other was Castillo San Juan), and here the island's troops would parade and be inspected. The centrepiece of the plaza is the appealing baroque statue of Our Lady of Candelaria, holding the infant Jesus and a tall candle. Formerly known as Plaza del Castillo, the square acquired its new name along with the statue.

At No 9, the Banco Español de Credito occupies the old Palacio de Carta: behind a rather dull façade this is a fine 18th-century mansion with carved wooden balconies and an elegant patio, immaculately restored by the bank. Originally built as the family home of Captain Matías Carta, it is now one of the best examples of traditional Canarian domestic architecture. Open during bank hours, it deserves a look inside, perhaps when you need to change money.

✉ West of Plaza de España 🍴 Bars and cafés in the square (€–€€)
↔ Iglesia de San Francisco (➤ 48)

# DISCOVER THE NORTH

## CASA DE CARTA (➤ 32–33)

## CASA DEL VINO LA BARANDA

Usually known simply as the Casa del Vino, this superb
*bodega* (wine cellar) situated in a converted 17th-century
farmhouse makes an enjoyable and educational outing – and
a great excuse to stock up on a few bottles of local wine.
Payment of a small charge enables visitors to taste any 10 of
the 150 wines stocked here. Not simply a shop, it sets out to
inform tourists about the range and qualities of Tenerife wines.

The building houses a small wine museum. It also shows a
10-minute film on the history of wine making on the island,
and explains why here, as in many other wine regions, quality
has much improved in recent years.

✉ 1km from Autopista del Norte, at Km 21 (Exit 13, El Sauzal)
☎ 922 572535 🕐 Tue–Sat 10–10, Sun and hols 11–6 (wine tastings
until 10) 🍴 Restaurant on site (€€) ☎ 922 563388 🚌 101
Puerto–Santa Cruz; 012 from La Laguna ♿ Few 💰 Free (charge for
tastings) 🔄 El Sauzal (➤ 66)

### BAJAMAR

One of the oldest resorts on Tenerife, Bajamar is a sharp contrast with the glitzier newcomers on the sunny south coast and has a loyal following. Here on the extreme northern shores of the island, constant breezes and turbulent currents stir up the waves onto the black beach. For that reason bathers rarely venture into the sea. Instead, visitors do most of their swimming and sunbathing at the seashore lido and hotel pools. It's also a quieter, less crowded, less developed holiday environment – precisely what attracts its devotees. Once a fishing village, Bajamar has few signs of its past, and now seems unfocused, with a long promenade and side turns, with many bars, restaurants and shops.

✉ 15km northwest of La Laguna 🚌 105 (Santa Cruz–Bajamar) every 30 mins 🍴 Variety of bars and restaurants (€–€€) ↔ Punta del Hidalgo (➤ 83), La Laguna (➤ 69)

## EL SAUZAL

This community has pretty terraced gardens and attractive homes, as well as an unusual domed church in Moorish style, the Iglesia de San Pedro. Its greatest attractions are its wine museum (Casa del Vino ➤ 63) and the exceptional coastal view, especially from the Mirador de la Garañona, which gazes along the sheer cliffs dropping into the sea. A little further along the road, Tacoronte is noted for its *malvasia* (malmsey) vineyards.

✉ 16km north of Puerto de la Cruz

🍴 Many fish restaurants (€–€€)

🚌 101 every 30 min. (Puerto de la Cruz–Santa Cruz); 012 from La Laguna ↔ Puerto de la Cruz (➤ 94), La Laguna (➤ 69)

## GÜÍMAR

On the border between the green north and the dry south, Güimar lacks charm but is an authentic Tenerife community with few tourists. Up the slope behind the town stand six curious large mounds, the enigmatic Tenerife step pyramids. Ancient Güimar was a place of importance to the Guanches; it's certain that the chieftain at Güimar had high status, for that was still true when Spanish colonists first began to settle here.

First studied in 1990 by Norwegian explorer Thor Heyerdahl, the six rectangular mounds were once deemed to be no more than piles of volcanic stones cleared from nearby fields by the locals. However, Heyerdahl's excavations showed that the structures are carefully built, arranged in large steps, with a smaller staircase climbing to a ceremonial platform on top. They are aligned with the summer and winter solstices, and closely resemble similar structures in Egypt and Mexico. This adds evidence to the theory that the Guanches were Berbers strongly influenced by ancient Egypt, but more tentatively suggests the Canaries were part of a prehistoric transatlantic route.

The pyramid area is now enclosed within an **ethnographic park**, with a visitor centre, Casa Chacona. One pyramid has been restored and visitors can decide for themselves what to make of the mystery, which archaeologists are still studying.

✉ About 23km southwest of Santa Cruz, and 3km inland from the coastal highway 🍴 Bars in the town (€) 🚌 120 from Santa Cruz every 30 min. ↔ Candelaria (➤ 74) ❓ Popular carnival first week of Feb; ancient midsummer festival in Jun

**Pyrámides de Güímar Parque Etnográfico**
✉ Calle Chacona ☎ 922 514510 🕐 Daily 9.30–6 ♿ Good
✋ Expensive

## LA LAGUNA

**Outwardly unappealing, the island's second city is a big, sprawling town rapidly spreading towards Santa Cruz, which is only 8km away. Like the capital, La Laguna also has a life and an economy that does not depend upon tourism. Many islanders work here, and there's a thriving university, giving the town a lively, youthful Spanish energy.**

La Laguna dates back to 1496, when *conquistador* Alonso Fernández de Lugo set it up as the island's capital, which it remained until 1723. The name means The Lagoon, but there is no lagoon here now (the town is properly known as San Cristóbal de la Laguna). The secret of the town is its exquisite historic quarter, where many fine 16th- and 17th-century Renaissance mansions survive.

It is rewarding to take a leisurely walk around the old quarter. To see most of the sights, stroll along Calle Obispo Rey Redondo from Plaza del Adelantado to Iglesia de Nuestra Señora de la Concepción (► 34), and back along parallel Calle San Agustín.

## CALLE SAN AGUSTÍN

In this delightful old-fashioned street parallel to Calle Obispo
Rey Redondo, look out for the Instituto de Canarias Cabrera
Pinto (Cabrera Pinto Institute of Canarian Studies), noted for its
exquisite traditional patio and handsome bell tower. The fine
17th-century façade next door, of the San Agustín monastery,
is an empty shell – the building was destroyed by fire in 1963.

✉ Calle San Agustín 🍴 In Plaza del Adelantado (€)


## CATEDRAL

The town's large cathedral is older than it appears. Founded in
1515, it was subsequently enlarged and a neoclassical façade
was added in 1813. This last feature survives but the
remainder was radically rebuilt during the early 20th century.
Nevertheless the dim interior contains a gilded baroque
retable (*retablo*), while set back from the high altar is the
unostentatious tomb of the island's conqueror and the town's
founder, Alonso Fernández de Lugo, buried here in 1525.

✉ Plaza de la Catedral 🕐 Mon–Sat 8–1, 5–7.30. Sun open for Mass
only 👤 Free

## IGLESIA CONVENTO SANTA CATALINA

The latticework gallery of the Santa Catalina Convent Church, beside the town hall, is one of several attractive architectural features. Inside, the former convent church has a silver-covered altar and baroque *retablos*. Notice the little revolving hatch near the side

entrance in Calle Dean Palahi, used by mothers who once wished to abandon their newborn girl babies by 'donating' them anonymously to the convent, to be brought up as nuns.

✉ Plaza del Adelantado 🕐 Mon–Sat 7–11.45, Sun 6.30–8 🖐 Free
🍴 In Plaza del Adelantado (€)

### IGLESIA DE NUESTRA SEÑORA DE LA CONCEPCIÓN (▶ 34–35)

### MUSEO DE LA CIENCIA Y EL COSMOS (MUSEUM OF SCIENCE AND THE COSMOS)

This fascinating and entertaining museum sets out to show the connection between man and the earth, and between the earth and the rest of the universe. With a variety of hands-on exhibits and displays, visitors learn about galaxies, our solar system and the human body, complete with such diversions as listening to the sound of a baby in the womb, taking a lie-detector test and watching a skeleton ride a bicycle.

✉ Calle Vía Láctea, off La Cuesta road, near university ☎ 922 315265
🕐 Tue–Sun 9–7 (shorter hours winter) 🖐 Moderate (Sun free)

## NUESTRA SEÑORA DE LA CANDELARIA, BASÍLICA DE

The Basilica of Our Lady of Cadelaria is dedicated to the patron saint of the Canary Islands. Profoundly revered, she is always depicted holding the Child in her right arm and a candle in her left hand. Spiritually, her role is as the symbolic bringer of Christian light to the darkness of Guanche life, and so she represents the rightness and justice of the Spanish occupation of the islands. The legend told by early Spanish settlers – not by the Guanches – was that over a century before the arrival of the first Spanish *conquistadores* the Guanches found a statue of the Virgin and Child set up in a seaside cave. Many legends claim the statue worked miracles to prevent the Guanches from harming her, and that the overawed Guanches began to worship the figure, which they called Chaxiraxi. In a mix of fact and fancy, it is related that the *mencey* (chieftain) of the Guanches welcomed the Spanish here, but that the Guanches were already Christians when the conquerors arrived.

The huge modern Basílica de Nuestra Señora de la Candelaria (1958), set back from the sea, dominates the small town. Inside, the statue of the Virgin sits enthroned in a glorious gilt setting behind the altar, among devotional murals. The statue dates from about 1830, what became of the Guanches' Chaxiraxi is the stuff of myth.

In the big sea-facing plaza outside stand sturdy, dignified, sad statues, representing the Guanche chiefs who were the rulers of the island before the coming of the Spanish.

✉ On the coast 17km south of Santa Cruz, Plaza de la Basílica, Candelaria 🕐 Daily 7.30–1, 3–7.30 ♿ Few 🚻 Free 🍴 Bars and restaurants in the town centre (€–€€) 🚌 122, 123, 124, 127, 131 from Santa Cruz 🚋 Santa Cruz (➤ 44) ❓ Festival of the Virgin of Candelaria 15 Aug, celebrated throughout the Canary Islands

## MUSEO DE HISTORIA DE TENERIFE
## (MUSEUM OF TENERIFE HISTORY)

The Casa Lercaro on Calle San Agustín is a grandiose 16th-century colonial mansion, and is the ideal setting for this impressive treasurehouse of island history. In an overview of Tenerife's story since the arrival of the Spanish, the collections include historical maps and maritime exhibits, and displays that take the story right up to the present.

✉ Calle San Agustín 22  ☎ 922 825949  ⏰ Tue–Sun 9–7  ♿ Few
✋ Cheap

## PLAZA DEL ADELANTADO

The heart of old La Laguna is a pleasant, shaded square where locals relax on benches enclosed by some of the most striking historic and dignified buildings in town, including the Ayuntamiento (Town Hall) and the Santa Catalina church (► 72) – as well as beautiful mansions adorned with fine porches and balconies. There are bars here too, and the town's busy Mercado Municipal (main market), with its lattice gallery, is the place to join locals in the morning stocking up with fruit and vegetables.

✉ Mercado Municipal, Plaza del Adelantado ☎ 922 258774
🕐 Mon–Sat 8–1 🍴 *Tapas* bars around the square (€)

## LAS MONTAÑAS DE ANAGA (ANAGA MOUNTAINS)

Tenerife's northern range of soaring, wild mountains remains remarkably unspoiled and is an ideal region for rambling and exploring well off the beaten track. Narrow, twisting roads give access to dramatic landscapes, while for walkers it is possible to see villages reached only on rough tracks. Here a simple subsistence life continues without any modern conveniences.

Long-distance paths have been waymarked by ICONA, the Spanish conservation agency. The ICONA signposting is clear, so you're not likely to get lost. However, it is unwise to walk without a detailed map. Walking maps can be obtained at the Puerto de la Cruz and Santa Cruz tourist offices and guided walks through the Anaga region can be organised. There is an information centre at the Mirador Cruz del Carmen, where maps and pamphlets giving details of set walks are available.

Part of the region has been designated a protected area, the Parque Rural de Anaga. Yet though impressive and steep, the peaks are not high – Taborno, the highest point, reaches only 1,024m, and a road follows the crests, giving superb views from a string of *miradores* (viewpoints), the most accessible is the Mirador de Jardina, near La Laguna). However, the exposed northern terrain is often misty, wet or even lightly snow covered on winter days.

✉ North of Santa Cruz 🍴 Mirador Cruz del Carmen (€€) 🚌 245, 246, 247 from Santa Cruz ↔ La Laguna (➤ 69), Santa Cruz (➤ 44)

## MUSEO DE ANTROPOLOGÍA, CASA DE CARTA (➤ 32–33)

drive

Allow a full day to explore the mountainous northern reaches of the island. This is the part with big working towns on the coast and in the valleys, simple hamlets scattered across the upper slopes, with breathtaking panoramic views from the hill crests. Begin the drive at Santa Cruz, or join at Tacoronte or at any point on the route if coming from the west or south.

*Head north for 8km on the coastal highway to San Andrés and the Playa de las Teresitas (▶ 82). Turn inland for 10km on TF112, the twisting, road to Mirador El Bailadero.*

You're now climbing into the Anaga Mountains (▶ 78). El Bailadero is a magnificent viewpoint, with sweeping vistas.

*Take the high cumbre (ridge or crest) road, TF1123, towards Mount Taborno. At the fork after 7km, take the summit road.*

A succession of views along this high road includes Mount Taborno's spectacular Mirador Pico del Inglés (a few metres up a side turn on the left). Continue along the crest road, with more viewpoints, notably at Cruz del Carmen, where there is a

17th-century chapel and a restaurant.

*After Las Mercedes take the right turn at Las Canteras on TF121 to Tejina. At Tejina, follow TF122 as it turns left towards Tacoronte. 7km beyond Tejina, 1km after Valle de Guerra, pause at the Casa de Carta.*

The island's remarkable Anthropology Museum is set in the Casa de Carta (► 32), a restored 17th-century farmhouse. Continue on this road to Tacoronte, the wine town (► 66).

*Leave town on the eastbound autopista to return to Santa Cruz.*

**Distance** 90km **Time** 4 hours
**Start/end point** Santa Cruz
**Lunch** Mirador Cruz del Carmen (€€)

## PLAYA DE LAS TERESITAS

Despite its huge popularity, the appeal of Tenerife pre-dates the sun, sea and sand recipe of today's mass tourism. Most beaches are unattractive and consist of rough, dark volcanic material (which comes as a shock to some visitors). However, island authorities are aware of the lack and have created some artificial beaches. By far the most outstanding of these is the beautiful curve of Las Teresitas, created in the 1970s with 98,000cu m of sand from the Sahara desert. Ironically, it was created not in the tourist heartland of the south, but in the far north, where locals could enjoy it. San Andrés, at one end of the beach, is a working fishing village.

✉ San Andrés, 8km north of Santa Cruz 🍴 Bars and fish restaurants in San Andrés (€–€€) 🚌 910 from Santa Cruz; 246 (Santa Cruz–Almaciga) stops 3 or 4 times daily ♿ Few ✋ Santa Cruz (➤ 44), Anaga Mountains (➤ 78)

## PUNTA DEL HIDALGO

If you want to stay at a Tenerife holiday resort yet get away from it all come to Punta del Hidalgo. Located at the end of a small road on the rocky Hidalgo headland that projects into the Atlantic from the northern coast, it's exposed to wild seas and strong winds. The resort does have its following – it's popular with German visitors and well known as a good place to enjoy the sunset. Its hotels give a fine view over the sea and nearby Anaga Mountains. The resort is growing and gradually extending towards its similar neighbour, Bajamar (➤ 64).

✉ 20km north of La Laguna 🍴 Bars and restaurants in the resort (€–€€) 🚌 105 (Santa Cruz–Punta del Hidalgo) every 30 min ♿ Few ↔ Bajamar (➤ 64), La Laguna (➤ 69), Anaga Mountains (➤ 78)

# Where to eat & drink...
# The North

## BAJAMAR

### CAFÉ MELITA (€)

Specialises in desserts, pastries and rich cakes. Lovely views.

✉ Carretera General ☎ 922 540814 🕓 Daily 9am–11pm 🚌 105 (Santa Cruz–Punta Hidalgo) half-hourly

## CANDELARIA

### EL ARCHETE (€€)

High-quality creative Canarian cooking

✉ Lomo de Aroba 2 ☎ 922 500354 🕓 Mon–Sat lunch

## EL SAUZAL

### LA ERMITA (€€)

Accomplished fish, seafood and international dishes attract a varied clientele to this restaurant on the outskirts of town.

✉ Los Angeles 74, El Sauzal ☎ 922 575174 🕓 Lunch, dinner. Closed all day Wed and Sun eve

## LA LAGUNA

### CASA MAQUILA (€€)

Local specialities, properly prepared at this simple restaurant.

✉ Callejón de Maquila 4 ☎ 922 257020 🕐 Lunch, dinner

### HOYA DEL CAMELLO (€€)

International and Canarian favourites.

✉ Carretera General del Norte 128 ☎ 922 262054 🕐 Lunch, dinner. Closed early May, late Aug, Sun eve

### TIPICO LAS ROSAS (€€)

One of the big, lively eateries that draw locals and tourists. Herby roast meat, salads.

✉ Carretera General 87, El Rasario ☎ 922 297355 🕐 Lunch, dinner

## SAN ANDRÉS

The cluster of humble restaurants (€–€€) along the waterfront of this pleasant little harbour village serve seafood and the fresh catch of the day.

### SANTA CRUZ

### CAFÉ DEL PRÍNCIPE
(€–€€)

Sit out with locals and tourists and enjoy a drink, a snack or a complete meal.

✉ Plaza del Príncipe de Asturias ☎ 922 242675
🕑 Tue–Sun 9–midnight

### DE TAPA EN TAPA (€€)

A wide range of excellent, good value *tapas* served by friendly staff at this bar-restaurant.

✉ Paseo Milicias de Garachico 1, Edificio Hamilton ☎ 922 151025
🕑 Mon–Wed 12.30–5, Thu 12.30–5, 8–11, Fri 12.30–5, 8–12.30, Sat 1–5, 8–12.30

### EL LIBANO (€)

Lebanese restaurant serving falafel, pitta, houmous and shwarma, and tasty less familiar vegetarian and meat dishes.

✉ Calle Santiago Cuadrado 36 ☎ 922 285914 🕑 Lunch, dinner

### LOS TRONCOS (€€)
Among the very best restaurants in the capital. Noted for
Canarian cooking of a high standard, and Basque specialities.
✉ Calle General Goded 17 ☎ 922 284152 🕔 Thu–Tue. Closed Sun
dinner & mid-Aug to mid-Sep

### PARQUE MARÍTIMO CÉSAR MANRIQUE (€–€€€)
The lido, on the Santa Cruz waterfront offers a range of fine
eating places from a café to the more formal restaurants.
✉ Avenida de la Constitución ☎ 922 202995 🕔 Daily 10–6

## TEGUESTE

### CASA TOMÁS (€)
A simple, family-run restaurant west of La Laguna (by the
church in El Portezuelo). Cooking is homely and authentic.
✉ El Portezuelo ☎ 922 638007 🕔 Sep–Jul, Tue–Sun 12am–11pm

### EL DRAGO (€€€)
Classic Canarian cooking with a creative touch; specialities
include local cheeses, fish casseroles and rabbit in spicy sauce.
✉ Calle Marqués de Celada 2, El Socorro ☎ 922 150288
🕔 Tue–Sun lunch, Fri–Sat dinner. Closed Aug

# Where to stay...
# The North

### GÜÍMAR

#### FINCA SALAMANCA (€€)

Charming farmhouse in lush gardens. A barn contains an airy restaurant serving Canarian specialities and local wines.

✉ Carretera Güímar, El Puertito Km 1.5 ☎ 922 514530; fax 922 514061

### LA LAGUNA

#### NIVARIA (€)

In a town with few hotels for holidaymakers, the Aparthotel Nivaria is a possibility. No restaurant but close to all amenities.

✉ 11 Plaza del Adelantado ☎ 922 264052

### SANTA CRUZ DE TENERIFE

#### ATLÁNTICO (€)

Pleasant, Spanish-oriented hotel in the main shopping street. Defined as two-star, it is modest and adequately equipped.

✉ Calle Castillo 12 ☎ 922 246375; fax 922 246378

### MENCEY (€€€)
This elegant hotel is the chief among Tenerife's traditional five-star accommodation. In sumptuous colonial style, the hotel offers every possible amenity. Away from the city centre on the north side of the Ramblas.
✉ Avenida Doctor José Naveiras 38 ☎ 922 276700; fax 922 280017

### PELINOR (€)
A smaller, less expensive hotel in the heart of the city close to Plaza de España and aimed chiefly at Spanish visitors. Neat, comfortable rooms and a bar on the premises.
✉ Calle Béthencourt Alphonso 8 ☎ 922 246875; fax 922 280520

### PLAZA (€€)
In an agreeable square in the centre of the city, this comfortable, reasonably priced hotel makes a good city base.
✉ Plaza de la Candelaria 10 ☎ 922 272453; fax 922 275160

### TABURIENTE (€€)
Long-established hotel. Many rooms have views over Parque García Sanabria and the main sights lie within walking distance.
✉ Avenida Doctor José Naveiras 24 ☎ 922 276000; fax 922 270562

# The West

If the island is divided into two, north and south, then western Tenerife certainly belongs to the north – it is luxuriant, full of colour, life and history. Yet even so the west is something different. Here, away from the busy valleys and towns of the north, there is a sense of space and distance and a remoteness from Spain. The climate is hotter and drier, the land more visibly volcanic, the atmosphere more serene. The dominant feature is Pico del Teide, rising far above all else.

Tenerife's first tourists were drawn to Puerto de la Cruz, and smaller resorts formed to either side of it, clinging to the rocky shores, eventually turning the corner at the Macizo de Teno (Teno Massif) and heading down into the south. Those early holidaymakers belonged to a more refined age, and even today the western resorts retain a calmer, less unruly air and attract a more discerning crowd.

## PUERTO DE LA CRUZ

Simply 'Puerto' to old hands, Puerto de la Cruz was the first town on Tenerife to attract tourists – and for good reason. Ideally placed for both north and south, and yet standing at a distance from the workaday world of Santa Cruz, this historic port has a lovely setting. It made a perfect base for the best of leisurely, civilised sightseeing before the days of 'sun, sea and sand'.

The Port of the Cross (as the name means), built in the 1600s, grew into a major port after the eruption that destroyed the harbour at Garachico in 1706. Puerto is green and luxuriant with a an exquisite climate. The town clings to the seashore, the lush Orotava Valley rises gently behind and Pico del Teide is clearly visible beyond. Puerto is a vibrant, living community that does not depend only on tourism. Its million visitors a year are among the island's most discerning tourists, and enhance the town's charming, bustling atmosphere. After the advent of mass tourism, the new crowds were bussed south to purpose-built resorts, allowing old Puerto to keep its air of dignity. At the same time it has adapted to the changing needs of tourism, with numerous quality hotels, good shopping, sophisticated entertainment, a casino, pretty public spaces and the best family attractions on Tenerife. For sunbathers, its lido is one of the most appealing in the Canaries.

🛈 Plaza de Europa 5 ☎ 922 386000 🕐 Mon–Fri 9–8, Sat–Sun 9–1

## DISCOVER PUERTO DE LA CRUZ

### BANANERA EL GUANCHE

Both entertaining and informative, Bananera is set in an old banana farm (*bananera* means banana plantation). A video (every 20 minutes) explains the method of banana cultivation. The banana, you are informed, is not a tree, but a plant, and takes 16–19 months before it produces its first 'hand' of bananas. One of its many peculiarities is that each plant is both male and female, and reproduces without pollination.

Visitors then stroll along a route that takes them through various kinds of banana plants, as well as many other intriguing species. You'll see varieties as diverse as papaya, mango, the huge and ancient drago (or dragon tree) species, sugar cane, cotton, coffee, cocoa, peanuts, pineapples and more. Less familiar names include kapok and chirimoya (custard apples). The cactus garden has hundreds of cacti, while in the Tropical Plantation there is a wide range of fruit trees as well as datura, tobacco and chicle – the South American tree from whose milky resin chewing gum is derived. There are exotic flowers too, including elegant, vivid *strelitzia*, or bird of paradise

flowers, which have become a symbol of the Canary Islands.

Finally, before leaving, you're offered a free taste of banana liqueur (powerful – and sweet) and a ripe banana. Many interesting fruit and flower specimens and souvenirs can be bought in the shop, carefully prepared and packed for the flight home.

✉ La Finca Tropical (2km from Puerto de la Cruz on the road to La Orotava) ☎ 922 331853
🕐 Daily 9–6 ♿ Few
✋ Expensive 🍴 Bar on site (€), restaurants in town (€–€€€)
🚌 Free bus to Puerto de la Cruz every 20 or 30 minutes

## CASA IRIARTE

Tomás de Iriarte, born in this house on 18 September 1750,
numbers among the few Tinerfeños to have made a name for
themselves outside the island. His poetry, plays and essays,
and in particular his scholarly translations (for example, from
Latin into German), made him a distinguished figure in 18th-
century Spanish literary circles. He left the family home at the
age of 13 to continue his education in Madrid, where he
remained until his death in 1791. This house was once
considered an architectural treasure. It has fine traditional

carved balconies and a beautiful interior courtyard, still well worth seeing, even though the house is today a charmless souvenir craft shop with a low-key maritime museum upstairs.

✉ Calle San Juan, off Calle Iriarte ⏰ Mon–Sat 10–7 ♿ None
✋ Cheap

## CASTILLO DE SAN FELIPE

A sturdy little coastal fortification, the diminutive Castillo de San Felipe is named after King Philip IV of Spain (1621–65). It was during his reign that settlers began to construct Tenerife's first capital, La Orotava, and its port, Puerto de la Cruz. The Castillo dates from that period and it remains the best example in the Canary Islands of Spanish colonial style architecture. The building has been immaculately restored and is now a cultural centre. Concerts are often given here, providing the option for visitors of a pleasing change from the usual type of entertainment on offer. The Castillo also houses art exhibitions.

✉ Paseo de Luis Lavagi ⏰ Open for events and exhibitions ♿ None
✋ Variable 🍴 In Calle de San Felipe (€–€€) ↪ Playa Jardín
(► 109)

### ERMITA DE SAN TELMO

San Telmo (St Elmo) is the patron saint of sailors, and the seafarers of Puerto de la Cruz erected this simple waterfront chapel in his honour in 1626 (rebuilt in 1780 after a fire). It is also known as the Capilla de San Telmo (Chapel of St Elmo). Dazzling white but for a tiny bellcote, it stands in a lovely little garden surrounded by the noisy ebb and flow of tourists and traffic. Although the street outside is named after the church, as is a nearby beach, there is something that touches the soul in this humble place. Here fishermen gave thanks for having

been spared from the dangers of the ocean, while beneath the floor are buried some who were less fortunate, victims of a flood in 1826.

✉ Calle de San Telmo
🕐 Daily. Services Wed, Sat 6.30pm, Sun 9.30, 11am
🚻 Free 🍴 Nearby (€–€€)

## IGLESIA DE NUESTRA SEÑORA DE LA PEÑA DE FRANCIA

Puerto's main church, the Church of Our Lady of the Rock of France, was started in the 1680s and took nearly 20 years to complete – even then it lacked the pale angular bell tower, added as an afterthought some 200 years later. Standing among the tall palms and flowering shrubs near the elegant central fountain (in the shape of a swan) in Plaza de la Iglesia, the church possesses a sombre dignity. The baroque interior is decorated with some fine statuary, as well as an ornate altarpiece by Luis de la Cruz in a side chapel. The organ comes from London – it was ordered and installed in 1814 by Bernardo de Cologán, one of several Canary islanders of Irish origin. Notice, too, the striking pulpit: its wood has been painted to look like marble.

✉ Calle la Hoya, Plaza de la Iglesia ☎ 922 380051 🕓 Mon–Sat 3–7, Sun 9–7. Mass daily 8.30, 6.30, 7. International Mass (usually in English) Sun at 10 ✋ Free 🍴 Drink or snack on terrace of Hotel Marquesa, Calle Quintana 11 (€€)

### JARDÍN BOTÁNICO (BOTANICAL GARDENS)

One of the most enjoyable places to pass some time in Puerto is the exuberant, exotic and colourful Botanical Gardens on the edge of town. It's the perfect place to rest out of the sun, grab a cool moment of tranquillity, or enjoy a serene park-bench picnic. Here hundreds of intriguing plant varieties grow in profusion, set in a peaceful shady park of only some 2.5ha. In places, roots, branches and twisting trunks form a fascinating sculptural tangle. Almost everything in the gardens is a native of some other land, the focal point being a huge 200-year-old fig tree, brought here as a sapling from South America. Today it rears up on an astonishing platform of roots. Like the other plants, it has flourished in this foreign soil, in an unarguable testimony to the benign climate and conditions of the island.

The gardens were set up in 1788 by King Carlos III as part of an experiment to see if it was possible to acclimatise plants to live in other climate zones. The intention was to see if useful varieties growing in tropical colonies could be 'trained' to survive in the mainland of Spain. The question was reasonable at the time, for it was not known how or why plant species live only in certain parts of the planet. The correct name of the

Jardín Botánico to this day is El Jardín de Aclimatación de La Orotava (La Orotava Acclimatisation Garden).

The range of species is prodigious, and includes several hundred plant varieties – some of which can also be seen at the Bananera El Guanche (➤ 96). Pepper trees, breadfruit trees, cinnamon trees and tulip trees mingle with coffee bushes and mango trees. Lovers of exotic flowers will be thrilled by the splendid hothouse orchids.

Tropical plants that thrived in these gardens were then taken to similar Royal Gardens at Madrid and Aranjuez in Spain to see whether – after their spell of adapting to the climate in Tenerife – they could 'learn' to survive on the mainland. For most mainland Spain proved simply too cold in winter. It is now better understood that while some plants can prosper away from home others cannot; for most of the exotics, growing in the Jardín Botánico Tenerife was as far as they were willing to travel. Many other varieties that were brought here failed to put down roots even in Tenerife.

✉ Calle Retama 2, off Carretera del Botánico ☎ 922 383572
🕐 Summer, daily 9–7; winter, 9–6 ♿ Few ✋ Cheap 🍴 Hotel Botánico (€€€); no casual dress 🚌 Along Carretera del Botánico

## LAGO MARTIÁNEZ

As a traditional resort, Puerto de la Cruz had a major drawback in the new era of mass package tourism: it had no decent beach. The solution was this beautiful lido, designed by the inspirational Lanzarote architect César Manrique and completed in 1977. Manrique was also responsible for the Playa Jardín, also in Puerto de la Cruz, which he developed in 1992 (► 109).

Manrique, an internationally acclaimed modern artist, had returned to his native Canary Islands where he had been given a free hand to develop tourist attractions. He had strong views on mass tourism. and argued that it should be encouraged within strict controls and that facilities should be of the highest, most creative standard.

Marketed under various names (Costa Martiánez, Lido de San Telmo, Lido de Martiánez), the Lago consists of eight attractively shaped pools and a larger swimming lake, interspersed with refreshing fountains and islets of lush greenery; the complex has proved a great success. Waterside sunbathing terraces, shaded by palms, are laid out in white and black volcanic rock. Touches of art and humour are everywhere: a popular feature is a central lava isle which periodically erupts as a fountain.

✉ Playa Martiánez, Avenida de Colón ☎ 922 385955 ⏰ Daily 10–7 (last entry 5pm) ♿ Few ✋ Moderate 🍴 Several eating places on site (€–€€€) 🚌 Along waterfront ↔ Ermita San Telmo (► 100)

## LORO PARQUE (► 26–27)

### MUSEO ARQUEOLÓGICO (ARCHAEOLOGICAL MUSEUM)

Located near the old fishing harbour, this small archaeological museum is housed in an attractive 19th-century building. The collection relates to the ethnography of the Guanche people. Interesting permanent displays include early maps, ceramics, equipment used in farming, jewellery, weapons and information on mummification. The museum hosts temporary exhibitions.

✉ Calle del Lomo 9A ☎ 922 371465 🕐 Tue–Sat 10–1, 5–9, Sun 10–1 ♿ Few 🚻 Cheap (free Thu) 🍴 Eating places nearby (€), especially in Calle de San Felipe ↔ Plaza del Charco (➤ 110), Puerto Pesquero (➤ 110)

## PLAYA JARDÍN

In 1992 the Canarian artist César Manrique transformed the neglected rocky bay near the Castillo de San Felipe into a remarkable waterfront beach garden. The Lago Martiánez (► 106), nearer the town centre, was an earlier success of Manrique's.

The site was chosen partly because the coast is more sheltered here and has less dangerous currents. Dark sand was imported to form a glorious stretch of beach, heightened by magnificent gardens of flowering bushes, palms and exotics cultivated on the surrounding sand and rock. Rocks rising inland add a backdrop to the scene.

Offshore concrete wave breakers hidden beneath the water protect Manrique's beach and gardens from the power of the ocean. As a result, Playa Jardín has become become one of the resort's most popular beaches. It has been awarded a Blue Flag, a symbol of good environmental standards and safety.

✉ At the western end of town, near Punta Brava ♿ Few ✋ Cheap 🚌 102, 325, 343, 382 from the resort centre 🍴 In the nearby fishermen's quarter, especially Calle San Felipe (€–€€) ⟷ Castillo de San Felipe (► 99), Loro Parque (► 26)

### PLAZA DEL CHARCO

A *charco* is a pool or pond, and this animated raised square stands where once shallow waters collected from the sea and locals fished for shrimps. Now the plaza, with its ancient Indian laurel trees, is the very heart of Puerto's old quarter and full of life – with bars and cafés, buskers and strollers. The charming restored 18th-century Rincón del Puerto, on the west side, has traditional balconies and a courtyard, now occupied by bars.

✉ Off Calle Blanco, near the fishing harbour 🍴 Bars and restaurants in the square (€–€€) ↔ Puerto Pesquero (below)

### PUERTO PESQUERO (FISHING HARBOUR)

There's no more picturesque reminder that Puerto does not exist only for tourists than this small working fishing harbour, not far from lively Plaza del Charco. A low harbour wall of black volcanic stone encloses the little bay. Modest but brightly painted rowing boats are hauled up on the shore, where local men and boys gather to talk or work.

On one corner, beside the water, a handsome building of dazzling white paint and bare black stone is the former Casa de la Real Aduana – the Royal Customs House. Built in 1620, this small public office continued to function as a customs house until 1833. (It is not open to the public.) Behind are the 18th-century harbour defences that protected the town and port from raiders.

Across the street, Casa de Miranda dates from 1730. It's a fine restored house, once the home of Venezuelan liberator Francisco Miranda, and now a bar and restaurant (➤ 132).

✉ At the end of Calle Blanco 🍴 In Calle Blanco and Plaza del Charco (€–€€) ↔ Plaza del Charco (➤ 110)

Puerto still has an atmosphere of history and much of the central area of this graceful colonial town is pedestrianised.

*Start from Plaza de la Iglesia.*

This main square is dominated by the church (➤ 101).

*Take Calle de Cologán (away from the sea) and turn into the second right, Calle Iriarte.*

Reaching Plaza Concejil and Calle San Juan, you'll find the elegant balconied 18th-century house Casa Iriarte to the right, now a souvenir and craft shop and a minor naval museum (➤ 98). On your left is the Palacio Ventosa, with its tall tower.

*Continuing along Calle Iriarte, turn right into Calle Blanco.*

This brings you to Plaza del Charco, the pleasantly bustling and shaded heart of town (➤ 110).

*Take Calle de San Felipe from the northwest corner of the square.*

This street has unpretentious restaurants and traditional Canarian buildings of character. Turn right and right again into Calle de Lomo, for the Museo Arqueológico (➤ 108).

*Retrace your steps to Plaza del Charco, then turn left on Calle Blanco towards the sea.*

Here is Puerto Pesquero (➤ 110), the harbour, with the Casa de la Real Aduana (Royal Customs House) on one corner.

*Follow the main seashore road (Calle de Santo Domingo) eastward past Punta del Viento (Windy Point), eventually reaching Calle de San Telmo.*

Pause to admire the tiny Ermita de San Telmo (➤ 100). Continue to the Lago Martiánez (➤ 106).

**Distance** 1.5km **Time** 1.5 hours **Start point** Plaza de Iglesia **End point** Lago Martiánez **Lunch** *Tapas* bars (€–€€) and restaurants (€€)
✉ Plaza del Charco, Calle de San Felipe

## DISCOVER THE WEST

### GARACHIO (► 24–25)

### ICOD DE LOS VINOS

One of the highlights of a tour around Tenerife is the little town of Icod. Its main attraction is the gigantic Dragon Tree known as the Drago Milenario, the Thousand-Year-Old Dragon Tree (► 18). But Icod has other charms too. The Plaza de la Iglesia has a lovely 15th-century church, the Iglesia de San Marcos, containing a baroque altarpiece, a fine timber ceiling and a magnificent cross from Mexico, a masterpiece of delicate silverwork. A short distance away, the Mariposario del Drago (Butterfly Garden) is aflutter with colourful tropical butterflies. Icod is also known for its wines. Taste and buy them at shops near Plaza de la Iglesia, such as Casa del Vino or Casa del Drago.

🍴 Bars and restaurants nearby 🚌 354, 363 (Puerto de la Cruz–Icod) every 30 min

## LOS GIGANTES (▶ 28–29)

## MACIZO DE TENO (TENO MASSIF)

The volcanic basalt mountains in northwestern Tenerife are among the most ancient rocks of the island. Their unusual geology and flora, and the steep, buckled terrain make the Teno Massif a splendid place for hiking.

Masca, a mountain village perched above a deep gorge, was once remote and virtually inaccessible. Now a daringly engineered road has made it a popular excursion, with roadside restaurants providing dazzling views.

Another improved road leads west from the little regional centre of Buenavista del Norte to Tenerife's most westerly point, the Punta de Teno, a dramatic headland with a lighthouse, where the Atlantic breaks against black rocks. Buenavista del Norte itself has a pretty main square with some 18th-century mansions; the Church of Nuestra Señora de los Remedios has fine altarpieces and a notable *mudéjar* (Moslem-style) ceiling.

🍴 Bars and restaurants in Buenavista del Norte, Los Gigantes (▶ 128, 130) 🚌 Los Gigantes (▶ 28–29)

## LA OROTAVA

Puerto de la Cruz was originally built as the port for older and grander La Orotava, the hilltown just inland whose coat of arms still declares it to be a Villa Muy Noble y Leal (most noble and loyal town). A jewel box of balconied façades, pretty decoration, cobbled streets and beautifully preserved historic buildings, La Orotava is best explored on foot. Start with the wonderful views from Plaza de la Constitución. The towers and dome of baroque Iglesia de Nuestra Señora de la Concepción in Plaza Casañas are a distinctive landmark.

Calle San Francisco is the highlight, climbing the west side of town from Plaza San Francisco to Plaza Casañas. Casa de los Balcones (▶ 16) is its main attraction. Across the street the **Casa del Turista**, though less grand, is older dating from about 1590 but in the same style, and has a craft shop where demonstrations are given of making sand pictures, a feature of the town's Corpus Christi celebrations. Also along here, 17th-century Hospital de la Santísima Trinidad used to be a convent – the revolving drum set in the wall by the main door was used to leave unwanted babies to be brought up by the nuns.

Interesting museums in town include **Museo de Artesanía**

**Iberoamericana**, celebrating the artistic and cultural links between Spain (including the Canary Islands) and Latin America; Artenerife, or **Casa Torrehermosa** (➤ 206), showcasing the best of the island's arts and crafts; and out-of-town **Museo de Cerámica**, with 1,000 pieces of traditional pottery. All three are housed in beautifully restored historic buildings.

✉ 6km southeast from Puerto de la Cruz L Carrera Escultor Estévez 2 ☎ 922 323041 🍴 Modest restaurants and *tapas* bars in Plaza de la Constitución 🚌 101, 345, 348, 350, 352 from Puerto de la Cruz ↔ Puerto de la Cruz (➤ 94) ❓ Corpus Christi in Jun

**Casa del Turista**
✉ Calle San Francisco 4 ☎ 922 330629
🕐 Mon–Fri 8.30–6.30, Sat 8.30–5
♿ None 🖐 Free

**Museo de Artesanía Iberoamericana**
✉ Calle Tomás Zerolo 34 ☎ 922 323376
🕐 Mon–Fri 9–6, Sat 9–2 ♿ None
🖐 Moderate

### Artenerife, or Casa Torrehermosa

✉ Calle Tomás Zerolo 27 ☎ 922 334013 🕓 Mon–Fri 9.30–6.30, Sat 9.30–2 💵 Free

### Museo de Cerámica Casa Tafuriaste

✉ 4km west town centre at Calle León 3 ☎ 922 321447 🕓 Mon–Sat 10–6, Sun 10–2 💵 Cheap

**drive**

This day out takes in all the grandeur of Tenerife's volcanic heartland.

*Leave Puerto de la Cruz on the motorway heading towards Santa Cruz, but exit at junction 11 (Tacoronte) for La Esperanza.*

La Esperanza is popular for lunch and a walk in the high pine woods of the Bosque de la Esperanza, just south on C824. This road is the Carretera Dorsal running along the mountainous 'spine' of the island (▶ 124).

*Take C824 south from La Esperanza. The road rises through pine woods, often shrouded in clouds or mist.*

At a bend, a sign points the way to the Las Raíces monument, marking the spot where Franco met army officers to plan their coup. Pause at the Mirador Pico de las Flores and other viewpoints for views of the coast. Eventually the road passes the observatory at Izaña and enters the national park (▶ 122).

*Follow C824 to the junction with C821 and follow it to the left, continuing south.*

The Centro de Visitantes (► 123), at El Portillo pass, marks the entrance to the Caldera de las Cañadas. After 11km of volcanic terrain you reach the Pico del Teide cable car (► 20) and 4km further, the parador, nearly opposite Los Roques de García (► 124).

*At Boca del Tauce, the typical Cañadas scenery abruptly ends. Return through the park to the Centro de Visitantes at El Portillo.*

Beyond El Portillo, take the left-hand fork down into the Valle de la Orotava, passing through heath, vines and bananas.

*Continue the descent into Puerto de la Cruz.*

**Distance** 145km **Time** 4 hours **Start/end point** Puerto de la Cruz
**Lunch** Restaurants near El Portillo and the *parador*

## PARQUE NACIONAL DEL TEIDE
## (TEIDE NATIONAL PARK)

**The Guanche name for Pico del Teide, the immense volcano rising at the heart of the island, was 'Tenerife'. For them, the mountain was the island, though in geological terms that's only partly correct. It was the emergence of this volcano, along with the Anaga and Teno ranges, that created Tenerife and subsequently shaped the island's terrain and dominated its natural and cultural development.**

While the northern fringes of the island are fertile and inhabited, the landscape around Pico del Teide remains harsh and unyielding. In particular, the area within the Caldera de las Cañadas, the remnants of a far bigger volcano whose eroded walls enclose Pico del Teide, is an awesome combination of rock and dust. In 1954 the surroundings of Pico del Teide were made a national park, its boundaries roughly following the borders of the caldera. Covering 189sq km, the whole park

lies above the 2,000m contour. It is strictly protected from any development.

The park can be visited by car, by coach (especially on through road C821), or by bike or on foot on numerous smaller tracks and paths. A cable car (*teleférico*) runs up Pico del Tiede to a point 163m below the summit (► 20). The cable-car station is 4km from the parador.

The visitor centre at the high El Portillo pass, east of Pico del Teide on the park through road, provides an introduction to the national park. For walkers, detailed maps of the park are available and excellent free guided walks set out from here (reserve a place by telephoning at least a day ahead).

🕓 Always accessible by road or on foot 🖐 Free 🍴 Restaurants (€€) at visitor centre or the *parador* 🚌 348 leaves Puerto de la Cruz once daily at 9.15, arrives at *parador* 11.30; return trip 4. 342 leaves Playa de las Américas once daily 9.15, arrives El Portillo 11.45; return trip 3.15

## CUMBRE DORSAL

Of all the routes to the Teide National Park, the most spectacular is the Carretera Dorsal road (C824), along the crest of the Cumbre Dorsal – the uplands that run northeast from the national park to the Anaga Mountains. Their slopes rise behind the Orotava Valley, with wonderful views to the sides and ahead. Along the road a number of *miradores* make unmissable stopping points (➤ 120).

## LAS CAÑADAS

This spectacular caldera, a crater zone measuring some 16km across, consists of lava fields, sandy plateaux (*cañadas*) and several freakish natural phenomena. One in particular, Los Roques de García, comprises a majestic cluster of misshapen rocks, easily spotted just opposite the *parador*. A waymarked walk goes round the Roques and is planted with various local flowers. To the north looms the awesome peak of Teide itself (➤ 20), while to the south lies the arid, sandy plain known as the Llano de Ucanca.

Another impressive rock formation is Los Azulejos (by the roadside about 1km south of Los Roques de García). This geological curiosity takes its name from the brilliant blue-green colorations of the rocks (*azulejos* is Andalucian for glazed tiles), caused by deposits of iron and copper mineral salts.

✉ Near C821 just south of the *parador* 🍴 The visitor cente at El Portillo has a choice of bars and restaurants (€–€€€)
🚌 348 once daily each way from Puerto de la Cruz to the *parador*. 342 once daily stops here from Playa de las Américas
♿ Free ❓ Choose clear, calm weather and come early to avoid the crowds

## PAISAJE LUNAR (LUNAR LANDSCAPE)

Accessible only on foot, this area of the park is a bizarre visual phenomenon. Here, high in the midst of nowhere, strange columns and shapes of tufa make a weird unearthly landscape. To reach the Lunar Landscape area involves an 11km round trip on marked footpaths just east of the *parador*.

The ascent of Pico del Teide is the most exhilarating walk on Tenerife – though it's only suitable for fit, experienced ramblers. Take plenty of water and warm clothes, and start as early as possible, checking the weather forecast and that the cable car is running for the return journey (► 20).

*Start from the main road C821 at the start of the track to Montaña Blanca.*

At first the track passes through a desolate volcanic terrain of sharp, gritty stones. After an hour or one and a half hours, you reach the old Montaña Blanca car park.

*Follow the sign indicating the Refugio de Altavista, which starts you on a steeper climb on a sandy track. Climb for about 2 hours along this path to reach the refugio, or mountain refuge – which may or may not be open (usually open daily 5pm to 10am). Continue on the path, the edge of which is clearly marked.*

Some 3 hours later, the path becomes stonier, but more level. Eventually you reach the path that leads from the top cable-car station to the summit. To complete the ascent you need a permit (➤ 23). You'll pass sulphurous steam holes emitting heat and vapour from the ground. The views are phenomenal. The summit is marked by a crucifix, where sometimes elderly local women come to say a prayer.

*Return to the cable-car station and take the car down to the road.*

**Distance** 8km **Time** 6–7 hours **Start point** From Montaña Blanca bus stop **End point** Top cable-car station (La Rambleta), or the summit **Lunch** Take a picnic – no food or water en route. There is a bar at La Rambleta (€)

# Where to eat & drink...
# The West

### BUENAVISTA DEL NORTE

### RESTAURANTE MESÓN DEL NORTE (€)

Enjoy the friendly atmosphere and traditional Canarian cooking at a reasonable price at Las Portelas in the Parque Rural de Teno area in the far west of the island.

✉ Portela Alta 1, 38489 Buenavista del Norte – Las Portelas
☎ 922 128049 🕐 Lunch, dinner

### GARACHICO

### ISLA BAJA (€€)

Respected due to its long-standing reputation, this rather pricey restaurant is located on the waterfront facing the Castillo de San Miguel. It specialises in good local fish dishes, though you can also stop for just a drink, snack or ice cream.

✉ Calle Esteban de Ponte 5 ☎ 922 830008 🕐 Lunch, dinner
🚌 363 (Puerto– Buenavista) hourly

### EL CALETON
(€–€€)

Perfectly located by the crashing waves on the waterfront facing the Castillo de San Miguel, this down-to-earth restaurant prepares

good meat and fish dishes in Canarian or international style, or you can just stop by for a soup, snack or ice cream.

✉ Avenida Tomé Cano 1 ☎ 922 133301 🕓 Lunch, dinner

## LA OROTAVA

### SABOR CANARIO (€€)

This charming restaurant is attached to the Museo del Pueblo Guanche in the heart of the old town – a showcase for Canarian crafts and food products. The restaurant serves authentic local dishes – try braised rabbit, roast cheeses or *ropa vieja* (literally 'old clothes', a classic Canarian hotpot). Head for a table in the plant-filled courtyard.

✉ Escultor Estévez 17 ☎ 922 322793 🕓 Mon–Sat lunch, dinner

## LOS GIGANTES/PUERTO DE SANTIAGO

### CASA PANCHO (€€)

This authentic restaurant comes as a surprise in a popular sun-and-sea resort area, catering mainly to British people on package holidays and with few signs of any indigenous local life. There's nowhere else quite as good for some distance around as this genuine Spanish restaurant serving tasty Spanish food to a high standard.

✉ Playa de la Arena ☎ 922 101323

🕐 Jul–May, Tue–Sat lunch, dinner 🚌 473 (Los Gigantes–Las Galletas, south of Los Cristianos)

### MIRANDA (€€)

Imaginative local and international cuisine in the heart of Los Gigantes. Light, modern decor and a good range of steaks, seafood and Canarian wines.

✉ Calle Flor de Pascua 25 ☎ 922 860207

🕐 Dinner

### TAMARA (€€)

Grandstand views over the resort and its giant cliffs give this restaurant much of its appeal.

✉ Avenida Maritima, Los Gigantes ☎ 922 862214 🕐 Lunch, dinner

## LOS REALEJOS

### EL MONASTERIO (€€)

At Los Realejos, in the hills above Puerto de la Cruz, this former monastery has been converted into one of the island's best restaurants, divided into a number of different rooms. Perfectly prepared traditional Canarian dishes include such classics as rabbit in spicy sauce with potatoes.

✉ Montañeta, S/N ☎ 922 344311 🕐 11.30am–midnight

## PARQUE NACIONAL DEL TEIDE (TEIDE NATIONAL PARK) (INCLUDING BOUNDARY AREA)

### EL PORTILLO DE LA VILLA (€–€€)

By the National Park Visitors' Centre, this large house at the El Portillo junction near the slope of the volcano has a choice of restaurants serving simple snacks and meals.

✉ On the main road TF21 at El Portillo, near junction with TF-24 ☎ 922 356000 🕐 Daily 9–4

### RESTAURANTE LAS ESTRELLAS (€€)

Out of the crossroads village of Chío, on the southwest side of the national park boundary, this bar-restaurant enjoys stirring views over the coasts.

✉ Carretera Boca-Tauce 21, Guia de Isora 🕐 All day 🚌 460 (Icod–Guía de Isora, via Chío) every 2–3 hours

### PARADOR LAS CAÑADAS DEL TEIDE (€€)

Spectacular *parador* close to Pico del Teide and all the major volcanic sites. The restaurant is unpretentious but correct, offers good food and is open to the public.

✉ Parque Nacional del Teide ☎ 922 386415 🕐 Lunch, dinner 🚌 343 (Playa de las Américas–Las Cañadas) once daily meets 348 (Puerto–Las Cañadas) once daily

## PUERTO DE LA CRUZ

### CASA DE MIRANDA (€€)

A cheerful *tapas* bar decked with gingham tablecloths, red chilli peppers and hams occupies the ground floor; upstairs its galleried, plant-filled restaurant makes a romantic setting for Canarian and international fare at reasonable prices.

✉ Plaza de Europa ☎ 922 373871 🕐 Lunch, dinner

### CASINO TAORO (€€€)

The casino restaurant attracts a dressed-up crowd and caters for them in style, with red-draped tables, formal service, smart atmosphere and a range of classy international dishes.

✉ Casino, Parque Taoro ☎ 922 372660 🕐 Dinner

### LA CASONA (€€)

Cook your own steak on a slab of hot stone at La Casona, one of the best of several Canarian–International eating choices in Rincón del Puerto.

✉ 13–14 Plaza del Charco ☎ 922 373422 🕐 Lunch, dinner

### LA CUADRA (€)

Enjoy a typical *tapas* snack or a hearty Spanish meal at tables set out on the main street leading down to Plaza del Charco.

✉ Junction Calle Blanco and Calle Iriarte ☎ 922 380271 🕐 Lunch dinner

### LA PARILLA (€€€)

Smart hotel restaurant offers top international and French-style cooking in an elegant setting. Dress is smart-casual.

✉ Hotel Botánico, Av Richard J Yeoward ☎ 922 311400 🕐 Dinner

### LAGO MARTIÁNEZ (€–€€€)

Several quality bars and restaurants provide snacks, drinks and complete meals in this lake and pool complex (➤ 106).

✉ Avenida Colon ☎ 922 381752 🕐 Daily 10–5, then Andromeda open until late

### MAGNOLIA (€€€)

Top-class dining at this restaurant attracts discerning locals and well-to-do Spanish visitors. Food is a mix of Catalan and international, with an emphasis on fish and seafood. You'll find the restaurant out of town in the La Paz *urbanización*.

✉ Carretera del Botánico 5, Avenida del Marqués de Villanueva del Prado
☎ 922 385614 🕐 Dinner

### MARIO (€–€€)

Choice eating establishment in the fine old Rincón de Puerto building, specialising skilfully in fish dishes.

✉ 12–14 Plaza del Charco ☎ 922 385535
🕐 Lunch, dinner

### PALATINO (€€)

An excellent range of seafood is served at this established restaurant in an elegant setting near the old fishing harbour.

✉ Calle del Lomo 28 ☎ 922 382378 🕐 Mon–Sat lunch, dinner. Closed Jul

### RANCHO GRANDE (€)

Bustling waterfront café in an attractive and convenient location for a quick bite. Cakes, drinks, snacks and inexpensive meals are available to eat in or take out.

✉ Calle San Telmo 10 ☎ 922 383752 🕐 Daily from 10am

## SANTA URSULA

### LOS CORALES (€€)

Enjoy fine food and wonderful views at one of the best of several good little restaurants in this area around 10km north of Puerto. Fish and shellfish excel on a menu of international and Canarian dishes, and there's an exceptional wine list. There is a room for those who just want *tapas* or a snack.

✉ Cuesta de la Villa 130 ☎ 922 301918 🕐 Tue–Sat lunch, dinner

# Where to stay…
# The West

### GARACHICO
### SAN ROQUE (€€€)
One of the most unusual and delightful hotels on the island, this historic building stands in the middle of the waterfront.
✉ Calle Esteban de Ponte 32 ☎ 922 133435; fax 922 133406

### EL TANQUE
### CASERÍO LOS PARTIDOS (€)
This retreat appeals primarily to walkers and visitors who value peace and quiet. A car is essential.
✉ Los Partidos 4, El Tanque-San José de los Llanos ☎ 922 693090; fax 922 693138

### LA OROTAVA
### VICTORIA (€€)
A 17th-century Canarian mansion in the old quarter restored in period style.
✉ Calle Hermano Apolinar 8 ☎ 922 331683; fax 922 320519

## LOS GIGANTES

### TAMAIMO TROPICAL (€€)

Large but secluded complex near the Los Gigantes marina and the fine beach of Playa de la Arena.

✉ Calle Hondura, Puerto de Santiago ☎ 922 860638; fax 922 860761

## PARQUE NACIONAL DEL TEIDE (TEIDE NATIONAL PARK)

### PARADOR DE LAS CAÑADAS DEL TEIDE (€€€)

Tenerife's only *parador* occupies a stunning location near the foot of Pico del Teide and makes an exceptional touring and walking base.

✉ Parque Nacional del Teide ☎ 922 386415; fax 922 382352

## PUERTO DE LA CRUZ

### ATLANTIS PLAYA (€€)

A reliable, very comfortable four-star high-rise holiday hotel close to the town centre. The bedrooms are attractively equipped.

✉ Avenida Venezuela ☎ 922 374545; fax 922 382153

# The South

The climate that caused Spanish colonists to stay in the green north of the island is the very thing that has caused foreign tourists to flock to the south. Everything beyond the lee of Pico del Teide is bone dry, a land stripped bare by Saharan sun. The light is dazzlingly pure and clear, the hills casting magical views across the emptiness to a perfect blue sea. For centuries this was the least valuable part of the island, in places little more than a desert. Up on the slopes some simple, remote shepherd villages survived, while down on the coast the harbour of Los Cristianos benefited from its sheltered position out of the wind. Now, though, the south is full of life and entertainment. Today that once-empty southern coast harvests Tenerife's most valuable crop: sun-seeking tourists. And for them, there can be no better place to be on this island.

## COSTA ADEJE, LOS CRISTIANOS AND PLAYA DE LAS AMÉRICAS

Los Cristianos effectively merges with Playa de las Américas, though it's less brash, more family orientated and has some Spanish character. The heart of Tenerife's package-holiday scene is a round-the-clock resort with a vast choice of accommodation, bars, restaurants and entertainment.

Surprisingly, the location is still beautiful, with rocky hills behind and attractions around the edges of town. The area extends westward from Los Cristianos through Playa de las Américas and into the newer district of Costa Adeje.

✉ Exits 27, 28, 29 or 30 of Autopista del Sur 🍴 Tourist restaurants (€–€€€) near beaches and close to Puerto Colón and Los Cristianos harbour 🚌 111 to Santa Cruz. Frequent services to all southern resorts; collect timetable from any tourist office. TITSA bus information ☎ 922 531300

## DISCOVER COSTA ADEJE, LOS CRISTIANOS AND PLAYA DE LAS AMÉRICAS

### AQUAPARK
A hugely popular waterpark with pools, rides, slides, flumes, wild water and dolphin displays. Many families, especially those with younger children, prefer to base themselves here throughout their stay.

✉ Exit 29 of Autopista del Sur ☎ 922 715266 🕐 Daily 10–6
🖐 Expensive 🍴 On site (€–€€) 🚌 Free from southern resorts

### COSTA ADEJE

Extending north from Playa de las Américas and the Playa de
Troya, this vast and still-expanding development now extends
to La Caleta and beyond. Aiming upmarket, many of its newer
hotels are elegant neoclassical designs, with masses of marble,
pillars, tiles, lush gardens and state-of-the-art facilities.

Puerto Colón, a smart marina of ocean-going yachts, makes
a focal point in this huge and somewhat amorphous resort.

🛈 Playa de Troya, Avenida Rafael Puig 1, Adeje ☎ 922 750633; Playa
Fañabé, Avenida Litoral, Adeje ☎ 922 716539 🕓 Mon–Fri 9–5 (or 4)

### JARDINES DEL ATLÁNTICO BANANERA

Though a second best to the Bananera attraction in Puerto de
la Cruz (▶ 96), this one offers an opportunity to see, taste
and learn about bananas in a genuine banana farm. You'll also
learn about Tenerife's crops and and how Pico del Teide
distributes the rainwater that falls on the island.

✉ Exit 26 of Autopista del Sur ☎ 922 720360 🕓 Daily 10–6; last
admission 4.15 🎟 Expensive 🍴 On site (€€) 🚌 Free from southern
resorts

## LOS CRISTIANOS

As this was the only coastal town already in existence in the late 1960s, when sun-seekers arrived in the south, it was to this harbour that they came. Los Cristianos already had a few bars and a good natural beach, and owed its existence as a port to a sun-trap location well sheltered from the wind. Even with the subsequent massive growth, the town maintains its separate identity and a refreshing sense of reality which is sometimes lacking at the newer resort next door. The focal point is the bustling harbour area, from where ferries depart for La Gomera.

🛈 Centro Cultural (Casa de la Cultura), Calle General Franco ☎ 922 757137 🕒 Mon–Fri 9–3.30, Sat 9–1 🚢 Hydrofoil and ferry services to La Gomera. Boat trips from the harbour

## PARQUE ECOLÓGICO AGUILAS DEL TEIDE (EAGLES OF TEIDE ECOLOGICAL PARK)

Here's a lush, tropical park that kids will love as a change from the beach. Bird shows are the highlight – not just eagles, but condors, flamingos, pelicans and penguins number among the birdlife living here, while animals include crocodiles, pygmy hippos and tigers. If that's not enough to fill the day, the attractions on site include dodgem boats, a bobsleigh run and other rides.

✉ On Arona road, 3km from Los Cristianos ☎ 922 753001 🕐 Daily 10–6. Exotic bird show 11, 2, eagle show 12, 4 (subject to weather) ♿ Few 🍴 Expensive 🍽 On site (€€) 🚌 Free bus from resorts

## PLAYA DE LAS AMÉRICAS

Love it or hate it, you should see it. Look out for the restaurant signs that boast, 'No Spanish food served here!' One of the most successful purpose-built resorts in the world, Playa de las Américas started construction at the end of the 1960s and has become almost a byword for how *not* to develop tourism. Unfocused, sprawling, much of it frankly ugly, and attracting low-budget packages, it nevertheless rightly remains supremely popular for a fun and sun holiday. Investment in its beaches has greatly improved the quality of the sand, the weather is perfect, and there's no doubt that for those who want to start the day with a full English breakfast at lunchtime, swim and tan all afternoon, and disco dance all night, this is the place.

🛈 Centro Comercial, near Parque Santiago II complex ☎ 922 797668
🕐 Mon–Fri 9–3.30, Sat 9–1 🚢 Boat excursions from Puerto Colón

## DISCOVER THE SOUTH

### ADEJE

This appealing little southern hilltown is the starting point for walks to the Barranco del Infierno (► 154). Though quite unremarkable now, it was once a Guanche tribal settlement and later became the Tenerife base of the counts of Gomera, who had plantations here worked by 1,000 African slaves. Ruins of the counts' fortress, Casa Fuerte, can be seen, and there's a 16th-century church, Iglesia de Santa Ursula.

✉ 6km north from Playa de las Américas
🍴 Restaurante Otelo I (€€), Molinos 44 (closed Tue) 🚌 416 (Granadilla–Guia de Isora) and 441 (Los Cristianos–La Caleta) run via Playa de las Américas to Adeje every 30 min

## COSTA DEL SILENCIO

This resort at the island's southern tip was one of the first tourist developments, though its name has become rather incongruous since the construction here of Reina Sofía Airport. There are almost no proper beaches – just the odd shingle strip and a few coves – but several seawater swimming pools make up for the lack. Costa del Silencio includes Las Galletas, a former fishing hamlet with two small beaches and a waterfront promenade, and Ten-Bel, one of Tenerife's first purpose-built self-catering resorts.

✉ 8km from Exit 26 of Autopista del Sur 🍴 Las Galletas waterfront has bars and restaurants (€–€€) 🚌 467 and other buses (Playa de las Américas–Las Galletas) ↔ Los Cristianos (➤ 146)

### EL MÉDANO

El Médano, on the island's exposed southeast corner, has the best natural beaches, but is generally too windy for sunbathing to be enjoyable. This is the island's leading resort for windsurfing and International contests are held here. The resort itself, on the headland of Punta del Médano, lacks charm and is very close to the international airport. Unspoiled pale beaches extend south to the hooknosed volcano at Punta Roja.

✉ Exit 22 of Autopista del Sur, 22km from Los Cristianos 🛈 Plaza de los Príncipes de España ☎ 922 176002 🕔 Mon–Fri 9–2/3, Sat 9–1 🍴 Bars and restaurants on waterfront (€–€€) 🚌 470 and other buses (Playa de las Américas–El Médano) ♿ Few

### LOS ABRIGOS

A fishing village close to Reina Sofía Airport, Los Abrigos is noted for its first-rate waterfront fish restaurants and has two beaches. Behind the village the Golf del Sur development includes an excellent golf course.

✉ 3km from Exit 24 of Autopista del Sur 🍴 Paseo Maritimo (€–€€)

The Barranco del Infierno itself (entrance is limited to 200 per day, so book ahead) is the valley of a stream that rises on the southeastern slopes of the Teide National Park (over 2,000m above sea level). This walk covers the short stretch above Adeje, where the stream passes through a dramatic canyon. Wear decent shoes and start as early in the day as possible to avoid crowds and the heat (carry water).

*Start at Adeje (► 150). Take the road that runs uphill through its centre. Continue on the steep road that leads to the gorge path.*

At the entrance to the gorge the path is fairly flat. Notice the caves high in the rock face – Guanche mummies were found in them. The rocky scenery is dramatic. The stream is the only permanent watercourse in the south. In places the vegetation is green and lush. Further on, the gorge becomes narrower.

*The path crosses and re-crosses the stream, now no longer flowing through a gully.*

There are some steep sections, but the total altitude gain is only 300m. Finally the path arrives at La Cascada, a waterfall in three levels pouring into a natural pool, where it is pleasant to rest and swim.

*To return follow the same path back.*

**Distance** 8km **Time** 3–4 hours. (Arrive early or book ahead, as visitor numbers are limited.) 🚶 **Entrance fee**: €3 **Start/end point** Adeje **Lunch** Otelo I (€€) ✉ Molinos 44, Villa de Adeje

## PARQUES EXÓTICOS

An astonishing sight in the midst of so much barren terrain, this lush tropical garden east of Los Cristianos is truly exotic. The main attraction is Amazonia, a slice of tropical rainforest created inside a climatically controlled domed area; it's hot and muggy inside. Parrots, hummingbirds and 5,000 butterflies fly freely around.

Other attractions include a reptile house, a well-stocked cactus garden and a zoo park. Many of the animals are chosen with children in mind and include friendly marmosets and squirrel-monkeys. You can even go inside the cages.

✉ Exit 26 of Autopista del Sur, 3km northeast of Los Cristianos ☎ 922 795424 ⏱ Daily 10–6 (7 in summer) 🍴 Restaurant on site (€€) 🚌 Free shuttle bus from Playa de las Américas and Los Cristianos ♿ Few 💰 Expensive ↔ Costa del Silencio (▶ 151)

## VILAFLOR

Quite unlike other settlements in the south, the prettily named 'flower town' is the highest village in the Canary Islands. Standing at 1,160m, it rises through cultivated terraces to pine forest on the volcanic slopes of the Teide National Park. The vines of Vilaflor produce drinkable dry white wines, and the village also has an abundant natural spring whose waters are bottled and sold all over the island. Although millions pass through Vilaflor on their way to the national park, few pause here and it remains unspoiled. On the village outskirts are a couple of *artesanía* centres, useful places to buy local arts and crafts.

Just outside the village, set back from the main road, the little chapel called the Ermita de San Roque stands by the viewpoint Mirador de San Roque. From here there is a majestic panorama across southern Tenerife down to the dazzling coast.

✉ On C821, 23km northeast of Los Cristianos 🍴 El Sombrerito (€€), Santa Catalina 🚌 342 from Playa de las Américas; 474 from Granadilla; 482 from Los Cristianos 🔄 Pico del Teide (➤ 20)

*drive*

Leave the resorts behind, climbing into sun-baked landscapes.

*From Los Cristanos take the Arona road, C622 (changes to C822 after the Autopista junction).*

Pass through the village of Valle de San Lorenzo to reach Mirador de la Centinela for views over volcanic cones.

*About 2km further on, minor road 5114 turns left towards Vilaflor. It climbs steeply in places, eventually reaching the 5112 at Escalona, where you turn right to continue climbing. The road skirts Montaña del Pozo (1,294m).*

Along here walled vineyard terraces climb the slopes to Vilaflor (► 157), noted for its white wines.

*At Vilaflor, turn left onto the C821 and keep climbing.*

Above the village, past the Ermita de San Roque, pause at the Mirador de San Roque for a tremendous view. Almost at once the road enters the pine forest that encircles Las Cañadas (► 124). A twisting mountain road through the forest gives more good *mirador* views as Pico del Teide comes into view.

*The road leaves the forest and at Boca del Tauce enters the volcanic Caldera de las Cañadas (► 123). Take a left onto the C823 for Chío.*

The road cuts across a landscape of cones and lava flows. Eventually you reach the pine forests once more. There's a pleasant picnic site and rest area (*zona recreativa*) near Chío. The road descends sharply. Before Chío there are good views down to the sea.

*At the Chío junction turn left and left again onto the C822. Pass little Guía de Isora. Cross a succession of barrancos (gorges), eventually reaching the Autopista del Sur. Take Exit 27 or 28 for Los Cristianos.*

**Distance** 106km **Time** 3 hours driving
**Start/end point** Los Cristianos
**Lunch stop** El Sombrerito (€€) ✉ Vilaflor
Las Estrellas (€€) ✉ Just before Chío

# Where to eat & drink...
# The South

## ADEJE

### OTELO I (€€)

Get a drink or a good meal at this modest, likeable bar-restaurant, brilliantly situated near the entrance to the Barranco del Infierno. It's especially popular for the island's traditional rabbit dishes, spicy chicken and Canarian specialities. Hearty portions and a pleasant atmosphere.

✉ Molinos 44, Villa de Adeje ☎ 922 710294 🕓 Wed–Mon 10am–midnight

## EL MÉDANO

### AVENCIO (€)

This reliable, inexpensive seafront favourite offers a cosy interior of rustic and nautical decor. Fresh seafood is always a safe bet, but there's plenty else on the menu. Catalan and Rioja wines accompany local vintages.

✉ Calle Chasna 6 ☎ 922 176079 🕓 Oct–Aug, Tue–Sun. Closed Sun dinner

## EL TANQUE

### MONTE VERDE (€€)

Located at a development further up the coast from El Médano, this restaurant offers a range of international, Spanish and Canarian cuisine that includes first rate steaks. There are tables set up outside, and a children's play area.

✉ Avenida Príncipes de España 2, El Tanque, Costa del Silencio

☎ 922 136502 🕓 Lunch, dinner

## LOS ABRIGOS

### LA LANGOSTERA (€–€€)

Drive past the Golf del Sur developments and down to the sea to find La Langostera. This is just one of a cluster of tempting little fish restaurants at this tiny waterside harbour along the Costa del Silencio. Enjoy the freshest and simplest of Canarian cooking, accompanied by good inexpensive wine.

✉ Paseo Maritimo ☎ 922 170302 🕓 Lunch, dinner

### PERLAS DEL MAR E HIJOS (€€)

Of all the fish restaurants lining the water's edge at Los Abrigos, this one has perhaps the best location, just above the waterline. Select your fish from the counter and specify how you want it cooked (steamed, grilled, fried). Terrace tables make a fine spot to watch the sun set over the waves and the planes landing and taking off from Reina Sofía Airport.

✉ Paseo Maritimo ☎ 922 170014 🕐 Lunch, dinner

## LOS CRISTIANOS

This resort has scores of tourist-orientated eating places, with more of them reaching a high standard of service and cuisine than is the case in neighbouring Playa de las Américas.

### LA CAVA (€€)

A breath of fresh air after a surfeit of bland tourist eateries, this establishment gives a chance to enjoy genuine, creative Spanish cooking in a pleasant outdoor ambience.

✉ Peatonal Cabezo 22 ☎ 922 790493 🕐 Lunch, dinner

### GOMERÓN (€)

Offering budget-priced unpretentious cooking, this functional restaurant by the bus station specialises in tasty Canarian fish and steak dishes.

✉ Avenida Juan Carlos 1 ☎ 922 751377 🕐 Lunch, dinner

### PAPA LUIGI (€–€€)

A cosy Italian restaurant in the town centre. The menu presents an extensive range of familiar variations on the themes of pasta and pizza, in addition to a selection of fish and meat dishes.

✉ Avenida Suecia 40 ☎ 922 750911 🕐 Lunch, dinner

## PLAYA DE LAS AMÉRICAS/COSTA ADEJE

There are hundreds of almost identical restaurants along the coast road through the resort. Their basic meals of pasta, pizza, paella, steak or fish and chips, and other international favourites are displayed in photos on boards outside.

### EL MOLINO BLANCO (€€)

A white windmill marks the spot, on the inland side of the resort. Though geared mainly towards foreign tourists, the rustic setting and welcoming atmosphere promise an enjoyable visit. Dining areas spill on to shady flower-filled terraces. Both wine list and menu are wide-ranging, with unusual items like goat or ostrich. Live music.

✉ Avenida de Austria 5, San Eugenio Alto ☎ 922 796282
🕐 Wed–Mon 1pm–1am

### EL PATIO (€€€)

Among the very best dining experiences on the south coast. Enjoy a high-quality Canarian and Spanish meal on the terrace of this hotel-restaurant near the Puerto Colón, where Playa de la Américas meets Costa Adeje.

✉ Jardín Tropical Hotel, Calle Gran Bretaña, Urbanización San Eugenio ☎ 922 750100 🕐 Dinner

### LA HACIENDA (€€€)

One of the elegant restaurants in the luxury hotel complex of the Bahía del Duque. Dress up for a memorable treat.

✉ Gran Hotel Bahía del Duque, Playa del Duque ☎ 922 746900 🕐 Lunch, dinner

### MAMMA ROSA (€€€)

This very popular restaurant demands a certain smartness from diners to match the good food, fine wine and professional service. Despite the name, the food is not exclusively Italian.

✉ Apartamentos Colón, Avenida Santiago Puig ☎ 922 792471 🕐 Lunch, dinner

### PORÍS DE ABONA
#### CASABLANCA (€€)
Leave the motorway at the Porís exit to track down this spacious pastel-toned restaurant near the seafront. Cuisine includes paella and home-made cheese.

✉ Carretera General ☎ 922 164296 🕐 Tue–Sun lunch, dinner

### SAN ISIDRO
#### EL JABLE (€€)
In this untouristy inland village near the motorway, close to the El Médano exit, there's an appealing and popular bar-restaurant serving hearty Canarian cooking.

✉ Calle Bentejui 9 ☎ 922 390698 🕐 Mon–Sat 1–4, 7.30–11. Closed Mon lunch 🚌 111 (Playa de las Américas–Santa Cruz)

### VILAFLOR
#### EL SOMBRERITO (€–€€)
El Sombrerito has a friendly, relaxed country restaurant serving authentic Tenerife recipes. Farm museum and shop attached.

✉ Calle Santa Catalina ☎ 922 709336 🕐 Lunch, dinner 🚌 342 daily from Playa de las Américas; 482 from Los Christianos; 474 from Grandilla

# Where to stay...
# The South

### COSTA ADEJE
#### JARDÍN TROPICAL (€€€)
Superb resort hotel in a seafront location.

✉ Calle Gran Bretaña ☎ 922 746000; fax 922 746060

### GOLF DEL SUR
#### TENERIFE GOLF (€€)
The seafront hotel stands near Reina Sofía Airport. There's a buffet restaurant, a seawater pool (heated in winter).

✉ Urbanización Golf del Sur, San Miguel de Abona exit of Autopista del Sur ☎ 922 237640; fax 922 738889

### LA ESCALONA
#### EL NOGAL (€)
A low-key, cream-washed, two-storey building, once part of an 18th-century estate, has been restored to create a small, charming hotel. Neat gardens surround a pool terrace.

✉ Camino Real ☎ 922 726050; fax 922 725853

## LOS CRISTIANOS

### TENERIFE SUR APARTMENTS (€€)

The accommodation consists of comfortable suites attractively furnished and well-equipped.

✉ Calle Amsterdam 3, off Avenida de los Cristianos
☎ 922 791474; fax 922 792774

## PLAYA DE LAS AMÉRICAS

### TENERIFE PRINCESS (€€€)

Located in beautiful landscaped grounds with a swimming pool and waterfall area.

✉ Avenida Antonio Domínguez Alfonso 6 ☎ 922 792990

## VILAFLOR

### EL SOMBRERITO (€)

A neat, well-managed village inn with agreeable, comfortably equipped bedrooms. The relaxed country restaurant downstairs serves authentic Tenerife recipes. There is a farm museum and shop attached.

✉ Santa Catalina 15 ☎ 922 709336; fax 922 709052

# La Gomera

Despite efforts to attract visitors, the tiny island of La Gomera has so far escaped the onslaught of mass tourism. A wild green landscape of plunging *barrancos* has made development difficult, just as it made colonisation impossible in centuries past. A new airport in the south may bring more people, but a lack of suitable facilities (though it does have two of the best hotels in the Canaries) ensures that La Gomera appeals mainly to those who need no entertaining, and want only to experience the simplicity and sun-warmed tranquillity of island life. Yet La Gomera offers walks, ancient woodland and a dramatic history. The island's capital, San Sebastián, is easily accessible by ferries crossing the 32km from southern Tenerife. Even for those who feel they must be back at their Tenerife hotel in time for dinner, La Gomera makes a most memorable day out.

Right: *Street scene in San Sebastian*

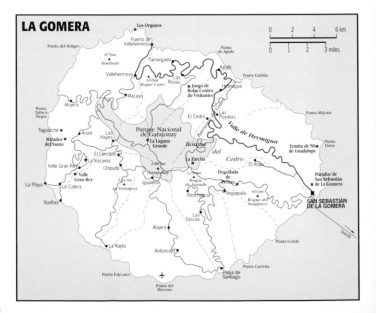

**LA GOMERA**

Los Organos
Punta del Peligro
Puerto de Vallehermoso
*876m Teselinde*
Tamargada
Punta de Agulo
Agulo
Punta Gabiña
Vallehermoso
Las Rosas
Hermigua
*650m Roque Cano*
Juego de Bolas Centro de Visitantes
Macayo
El Cedro
Las Poyatas
Punta Majona
Punta Talisca Negra
Alojera
Taguluche
Arure
Las Hayes
**Mirador del Santo**
Parque Nacional de Garajonay
**La Laguna Grande**
*Bosque del Cedro*
Valle de Hermigua
Ermita de NS de Guadalupe
Punta Llana
El Cercado
La Zarcita
El Atán
La Vizcaina
Chipude
*1484m Garajonay*
Degollada de Peraza
*663m*
Parador de San Sebastián de La Gomera
Valle Gran Rey
**Valle Gran Rey**
La Calera
*1241m Roque de Agando*
Vegapala
*Roque del Sombrero*
**SAN SEBASTIÁN DE LA GOMERA**
La Playa
Vueltas
Igualero
*1243m La Fortaleza*
Benchijigua
Las Toscas
Alajeró
Punta Gorda
La Rajita
Antoncojo
Tenerife
Punta Gaviota
Punta Falcones
Playa de Santiago
Punta del Becerro

0   2   4   6 km
0   1   2   3 miles

## AGULO

A pearl of a village in a delightful setting above the coast, Agulo is enclosed by a semicircle of steep green hills, pouring with waterfalls and streams after rain showers. The town's narrow cobbled streets are focused on a domed Moorish-looking church, while out to sea the inspiring vision of Pico del Teide rises above the clouds from the dark floating form that is Tenerife. It's one of the prettiest spots on the north coast.

✉ 27km from San Sebastián on the northern road 🍴 Las Rosas (€€) in Las Rosas hamlet, 2km west ↔ Hermigua (► 178) ❷ Fiesta of San Marcos 25 Apr; Los Piques mid–late Jun (*silbo* language)

## CHIPUDE

Until recently Chipude was a remote hamlet, lost high in the green heart of the island. Among Gomerans its name used to be synonymous with a rustic way of life and poverty, and locals say that the people of Chipude used to drive away intruders with stones.

While better roads and communications have changed all that, the villagers thankfully still preserve their old customs and traditions, and it is here that you may hear *silbo* – not being demonstrated for tourists, but used to call to friends or neighbours (➤ below).

Chipude has long been noted for its handmade pots crafted without a potter's wheel and decorated with traditional Guanche motifs, though in fact these are more often from the neighbouring village of El Cercado.

Legend has it that the extraordinary rock formation known as La Fortaleza, or the Chipude Fort, 2km south of the village, was a Guanche sacred site. This is easy to believe – its sheer stone soars vertically more than 1,200m to a tabletop crest.

✉ 29km west from San Sebastián, off the central highland routes
🍴 Village bars (€)  ↔ Parque Nacional de Garajonay (➤ 36)

## EL SILBO

Due to the need to communicate across steep terrain and dense forest the Gomerans developed a whole vocabulary, syntax and grammar of whistles. Another quality of *el silbo* is its volume: skilled *silbadores* can whistle a detailed message to another person several kilometres away.

## HERMIGUA

Lying in the island's most fertile and productive valley, Hermigua tacks along the road through plantations of banana palms. Though one of La Gomera's larger settlements, it's a tiny, tranquil place, a stopping point for visitors who want to see local crafts being made and maybe make a purchase at the interesting Los Telares *artesanía* (craft centre). Nearly opposite is the Convento de Santo Domingo, a 16th-century church with a Moorish-style wooden ceiling.

✉ 20km from San Sebastián on the northern road 🏨 Callejón de Ordaiz 161, Hermigua ☎ 922 144101 🍴 El Silvo (€), a simple bar-restaurant in the village 🔄 Agulo (► 176)

## LOS ÓRGANOS (THE ORGANS)

Inaccessible from the land, these strange slender columns of basalt emerging from the sea to the northwest of Puerto de Vallehermoso are so named because they resemble organ pipes. Extending over a 200m stretch of cliff, and rising as much as 80m from the sea, the tightly packed hexagonal columns make an impressive sight, and they certainly provide a good excuse for a boat excursion (see below for pick-up points). Surprisingly, they do look just like the pipes of some gigantesque organ.

✉ 52km from San Sebastián on north coast 🍴 Bars in Vallehermoso (€) 🚤 Only accessible by boat, either from Puerto de Vallehermoso (4km from Los Órganos), or on longer excursions from Playa de Santiago, Vueltas or San Sebastián 🔄 Vallehermoso (► 189)

## PARQUE NACIONAL DE GARAJONAY (► 36–37)

### PLAYA DE SANTIAGO

The southernmost point of La Gomera, close to the island's airport, is blessed with a sheltered position, good beaches and an attractive setting. A growing success as a resort area, it was traditionally a large and prosperous fishing and farming village that went into decline in the 1970s. In recent years it has been reborn thanks to new watersports, beach and harbour facilities and the building of the impressive and imaginative upmarket resort hotel Jardin Tecina by cruise operators Fred Olsen.

The old waterfront village is steadily expanding with the influx of bars and restaurants. At one end, a small fishermen's chapel decorated with model boats is set into the rock face.

✉ 30km southwest from San Sebastián 🛈 Edificio Las Vistas, Local 8, Avenida Marítima s/n ☎ 922 895650 🍴 Simple bars and restaurants on the waterfront (€–€€), Hotel Jardín Tecina (€€–€€€) ↔ Parque Nacional de Garajonay (► 36)

## SAN SEBASTIÁN DE LA GOMERA

La Gomera's capital, usually known as San Sebastián and often known to locals simply as Villa, is an unprepossessing little port, though it has an excellent harbour. In several ways San Sebastián is quite untypical of the island. Though hemmed in by hills, the town lies on flat ground while the rest of La Gomera is all steep slopes and valleys; its dusty, dry setting is a marked contrast to the island's exotic greenery. Most of the town is modern white cubes in an island full of rustic character. Only San Sebastián's picturesque main street, Calle Real (sometimes known as Calle del Medio), and the main square, Plaza de las Américas, with its balconied mansions, evoke the memory of colonial times and drama of the island's history.

La Gomera was the last Canary Island to be subjugated by the Spanish – it remained independent until 1837. As a result, no other Canary Island retains so much of the native Guanche culture and ethnicity. There are, too, visible in many island faces, reminders of the African slaves who were kept here.

When Christopher Columbus anchored at San Sebastián before the voyage that discovered the Americas, this was the most westerly port in the world. Tenerife remained in Guanche hands, while on La Gomera only this edge of the island was under Spanish control.

To recapture a little of that past, walk along the main street, Calle Real. Here is the 17th-century Casa del Pozo, once the customs house; the name means House of the Well. Inside is the **Pozo de la Aguada**, the well from which Columbus's quartermaster drew the water to supply his ships on the outward voyage to America. Here, too, the expedition bought seeds, grains and flowers to be planted in the New World.

In the same street stands the Iglesia Nuestra Señora de la Asunción (Church of Our Lady of the Assumption), where – we are told – Columbus said his last prayer before setting out on the great voyage. Founded in the 15th-century, the church was largely rebuilt in the late 18th century.

Also in Calle Real, Casa de Colón (Columbus House) has no proven link with the explorer, but is now claimed as the house where he lodged. It has been restored as a museum about Columbus and is the focal point of the town's annual week-long Columbus festival in September.

Finally, in the harbourside park, the Torre del Conde (Count's Tower, closed to visitors) is the oldest building in

continuous use in the Canary Islands. This sturdy tower house dates from 1447, and was once the residence of Beatriz de Bobadilla, wife of the count of La Gomera, Hernán Peraza (whose father had built the tower).

✉ On the east coast of island 🚹 Calle Real 4 ☎ 922 141512 🍴 Bars in town (€); good food at the Parador de San Sebastián de la Gomera (€€€) 🚌 The intermittent bus service is not reliable. Taxis are readily available at the ferry dock ↔ Parque Nacional de Garajonay (➤ 36) ❓ Fiestas include the local saint's festival around 20 Jan; Carnaval (Carnival) about the end of Feb; Semana Colombina (Columbus Week) 1–6 Sep; Virgen de Guadaloupe 1–6 Oct

## Pozo de la Aguada

✉ Calle Real ☎ 922 141512 🕐 Mon–Sat 9–1.30, 3.30–6, Sun 10–1 ♿ None 💷 Free ❓ In the same building as the tourist office

## VALLE GRAN REY

On the west side of the island, the majestic Valley of the Great King is still remote and was almost unknown until the 1970s, when it became something of a hippy retreat – offering an away-from-it-all, ecologically sustainable lifestyle. Today, though, and despite the location, it attracts more visitors than anywhere else on the island.

On the twisting road up to Arure (10km inland), several viewpoints offer stunning panoramas of cultivated terraces clinging to the lower slopes of the steep ravine, the scattered white houses of a few hamlets, and the valley opening out to greenery beside the vibrant blue sea. One hamlet has a spectacularly located *mirador* restaurant designed by Lanzarote architect César Manrique.

The road descends the ravine to reach La Calera, the attractive little central community of the Valle Gran Rey, standing among banana plantations. Beyond, the road divides for the last 1km to the sea: to the north is La Playa; to the south is the fishing harbour and port at Vueltas, the traditional gateway to the valley. Both settlements have simple waterside eateries offering the freshest of fish. La Playa and Vueltas have developed as tourist centres since the 1980s and their little shingle beaches are among the best that La Gomera offers.

✉ 44km from San Sebastián 🛈 Calle Lepanto, La Playa, Valle Gran Rey ☎ 922 805458 🍴 Many bars and fish restaurants on the coast 🚌 Occasional buses and boats from San Sebastián ❓ Los Santos Reyes fiesta 6 Jan (Epiphany)

## VALLEHERMOSO

An attractive and appealing village – one of the island's largest communities – Vallehermoso is indeed in a 'beautiful valley' as its name suggests. It is surrounded by forest, vineyards and palm plantations of date and banana. A striking 650m-high volcanic pinnacle close by is called Roque Cano, Dog Rock, supposedly for its resemblance to a canine tooth.

✉ 48km northwest of San Sebastián

🍽 Bar-restaurants in the village centre (€)

↔ Los Órganos (➤ 179)

drive

The deeply cut, forested terrain of La Gomera restricts access, and until recently most journeys were made by boat, around the coastline of the island.

*Start out from San Sebastián on the Hermigua road, TF711.*

The road climbs steeply up the Barranco del Cedro, giving views over the water to Tenerife, and passes by a large statue of Christ that overlooks San Sebastián.

*The road climbs higher and skirts the edges of the Parque Nacional de Garajonay (➤ 36).*

Here the road winds through unspoiled mixed woodland of laurel, beech, pine and flowering heather trees, despite the particular name for this area, Bosque del Cedro (Cedar Forest).

*After sharp turns and a tunnel, the road begins
descending towards the north coast.*

The road descends into Hermigua (► 178) and, 3km further,
Agulo (► 176).

*The road, winding all the time, climbs inland beside a
plunging green valley, passing Las Rosas restaurant and
continuing to Vallehermoso.*

At Tamargada, pause at a fine *mirador* to look at the forest. At
Vallehermoso (► 189) there is abundant cultivation of date
palms and bananas.

*A poor road leads down to the shore at Puerto de
Vallehermoso.*

From the harbour, regular boat trips go out to see the strange
rock formations of Los Órganos (► 179).

**Distance** 50km **Time** 2–3 hours **Start point** San Sebastián de la
Gomera **End point** Puerto de Vallehermoso
**Lunch** Restaurant Las Rosas (€€)

# Where to eat & drink...
# La Gomera

## LA GOMERA

### EL PAJAR DE VALENCIA (€)
Enjoy straightforward cooking of no-nonsense Spanish dishes as well as pizzas and other Mediterranean fare at this cheeful bar-restaurant.

✉ 26 Calle Ruiz de Padrón, San Sebastián ☎ 922 870355 🕓 All day

### EL SILVO (€)
Modest bar-restaurant on the main road just north of the village. Enjoy an inexpensive drink or meal with a view.

✉ Carretera General 102, Hermigua el Tabaibal ☎ 922 880304
🕓 Tue–Sun lunch, dinner

### HOTEL JARDÍN TECINA RESTAURANT (€€)
The terrace of this excellent hotel on La Gomera's south coast offers international dining and a wonderful view of the sea.

✉ Lomada de Tecina, Playa de Santiago ☎ 922 145850 🕓 Lunch, dinner

### LAS ROSAS (€€)

Not just a place to take lunch, this pretty roadside restaurant at Agulo is an essential stopover on a tour of La Gomera. Its superb valley-edge location and views and, most of all, its fascinating demonstrations of *el silbo*, the island's unique whistling language, attract coach parties every day. However, the delightful Canarian specialities served are very tasty, too.

✉ Carretera General, Agulo Las Rosas ☎ 922 800916 🕐 Lunch

### LA TASCA (€–€€)

An atmospheric old house in San Sebastián provides the setting for a popular, very reasonably priced restaurant offering a wide variety of international fare ranging from familiar, straightforward meals to more interesting spicy dishes and good salads.

✉ Calle Ruiz de Padrón 54 ☎ 922 141598 🕐 Dinner only

### PARADOR DE SAN SEBASTIÁN DE LA GOMERA (€€–€€€)

This *parador* (► 195) has the best food on the island; Spanish and international cuisine.

✉ Pista Llano la Villa, San Sebastian ☎ 922 871100 🕐 Lunch, dinner

# Where to stay...
# La Gomera

There are a limited number of hotels and *pensiones* on the island, most of the accomodation involves staying in homes or private apartments. *Casas rurales* are former farmhouses now converted to rental properties (☎ 922 595019).

## HERMIGUA
### IBO ALFARO (€)
Delightful rural hostelry is on a quiet track above a valley village. Breakfast is served on a terrace in fine weather.
✉ Hermigua ☎ 922 880168; fax 922 881019

## PLAYA DE SANTIAGO
### JARDÍN TECINA (€€€)
This top-class hotel clings to a clifftop, with magnificent gardens of native plants. rising in the distance. The 'rooms' are in delightful cottages in the grounds.
✉ Lomada de Tecina, Playa de Santiago ☎ 922 145850; fax 922 145851

### SAN SEBASTIÁN

## PARADOR DE SAN SEBASTIÁN DE LA GOMERA (€€€)

La Gomera's attractive *parador* stands high above the port up a steeply winding road.

✉ Llano de la Horca 1
☎ 922 871100; fax 922 871116

### VALLE GRAN REY

## JARDÍN DEL CONDE (€€)

This attractive apartment complex is brightly landscaped with lots of greenery and flowering plants.

✉ Avenida Maritima ☎ 922 806008; fax 922 805385

### VALLEHERMOSO

## HOTEL DE TRIANA (€)

Bedrooms feature mosaic-tiled bathrooms, and some have kitchenettes. A small restaurant provides simple cuisine.

✉ Calle Triana ☎ 922 800528; fax 922 800128

Shopping
& leisure

## WHERE TO TAKE THE CHILDREN

The island provides little that is especially for children, but it doesn't need to – most of Tenerife's attractions are a are a big hit with people of all ages.

## AMAZING PLANTS

### BANANERA EL GUANCHE

All about bananas – and other plants (➤ 96).

✉ 2km from Puerto de la Cruz, on road to La Orotava ☎ 922 331853 🕐 Daily 9–6

### DRAGO MILENARIO

One of the largest and oldest specimens of this curious tree (➤ 18).

✉ Icod de los Vinos 🚌 354, 363 from Puerto de la Cruz

### JARDÍN BOTÁNICO

Spot the giant South American fig tree in this exotic garden (➤ 102).

✉ Calle Retama 2, off Carretara del Botánico, Puerto de la Cruz ☎ 922 383572 🕐 Summer, daily 9–7; winter, 9–6

### PARQUE NACIONAL DE GARAJONAY
The twisting branches of the forest are like scenes from a movie (▶ 36).
✉ La Gomera

## ANIMAL PARKS

### LORO PARQUE
A wonderland of animals and birds (▶ 26).
✉ 1.5km west of Puerto de la Cruz, near Punta Brava ☎ 922 373841
🕔 Daily 8.30–5 🚌 Free shuttle from Avenida de Colón (near Lago) and Plaza del Charco, Puerto de la Cruz

### OASIS DEL VALLE
Canarian flora and fauna and other friendly creatures set in lush subtropical gardens in the Orotava Valley.
✉ El Ramal 35, La Orotava (Exit 33 from Autopista del Norte)
☎ 922 333509 🕔 Daily 10–5 🚌 Free bus from Playa de Martiánez (near Lago), Puerto de la Cruz

### PARQUE ECOLÓGICO AGUILAS DEL TEIDE
See condors and crocodiles, tigers, eagles and penguins in this dramatic tropical park (▶ 147).

✉ On Arona road 3km from Los Cristianos ☎ 922 753001
🕐 Summer, daily 9–6; winter, 10–6 🚌 Free shuttle bus from Playa de las Américas and Los Cristianos

## PARQUES EXÓTICOS

Cactus and animal park, and also a reptilarium (▶ 156).

✉ Near Exit 26 of Autopista del Sur ☎ 922 795424 🕐 Daily 10–6
🚌 Free shuttle bus from Playa de las Américas and Los Cristianos

## TENERIFE ZOO

Apes and other primates as well as lions, crocodiles and many other creatures.

✉ Llano Azul, Arona (Exit 26 of Autopista del Sur) ☎ 922 751753
🕐 Daily 9.30–6 🚌 Free shuttle bus from southern resorts

# CAMEL RIDES

### CAMEL PARK

A farm in the sun, breeding camels, making wine, growing local crops and selling island crafts. Mini-excursions by camel.
✉ Exit 27 of Autopista del Sur ☎ 922 732422 🕐 Daily 10–5 🚌 Free shuttle bus from Los Cristianos and Playa de las Américas

### CAMELLO CENTER

Hold on tight for camel rides and donkey safaris at El Tanque, near Garachico. Afterwards have tea in an Arab tent.
✉ El Tanque (east of Garachico) ☎ 922 136399 🕐 Daily 10–6

# MEETING WHALES AND DOLPHINS

Whale- and dolphin-watching are a popular activities. About 20 different species of sea mammals live in these waters, mostly off the west coast between Los Cristianos and Los Gigantes.

### ROYAL DELFIN

Choice of trips by modern glass-bottomed catamaran with a chance to see whales, porpoises and dolphins.
✉ Puerto Colon (Playa de las Americas) and Puerto de la Cruz
☎ 900 700709 🕐 Daily trips

## WATER FUN

### AQUAPARK (AGUAPARK OCTOPUS)

This water amusement park offers slides, pools, dolphin shows and water features. Plan to spend at least half a day; you can have a meal here too (► 143).

✉ San Eugenio Alto, Costa Adeje/Playa de las Américas (Exit 29 of Autopista del Sur) ☎ 922 715266 🕐 Daily 10–6 🚌 Free shuttle bus from southern resorts

## SMALL WORLD

### PUEBLO CHICO

Models of Canarian landscapes and buildings are carefully reproduced to a scale of 1:25 in this large open-air attraction in the hills behind Puerto de la Cruz.

✉ Valle de la Orotava ☎ 922 334060

# HANDICRAFTS/SOUVENIRS

## DUTY AND TAX

Although the Canary Islands are a duty-free area, it doesn't follow that all goods are free of tax. Prices are bumped up by the local IGIC tax, which puts 5 per cent on the value of goods and is sometimes not included in window-display prices.

## EMBROIDERY, LACE AND THREADWORK

The Canaries are known for exquisite embroidery (*bordados*) and fine threadwork (*calados*), and decorative lacework, especially doilies (*rosetas*). Exceptional patience, skill, delicacy and care are required of the local women who do the work. Beware of street sellers and market traders offering very inferior low-priced imported factory-made embroidery.

## POTTERY

On Tenerife and La Gomera highly skilled local potters still work by hand to produce distinctive household objects and decorative items (▶ 177). Look out in the craft shops for their *gánigos* (household pots made without a potter's wheel) and jewellery decorated with Guanche symbols.

## WICKERWORK

Local handmade Tenerife basketwork is distinctive and pretty, and makes a good choice for souvenirs. Skilled wickerwork craftsmen and women can be seen working in the craft fairs.

## SHOPS

A range of all these locally made items can be found at the following craft stores. It may be worth shopping around, as the stock varies from place to place. Shop hours are generally Mon–Sat 9–1, 4–8.

### THE NORTH

### ARTESANÍA CELSA
✉ Calle Castillo 8, Santa Cruz

### ART Y HOBBY
Exhibitions and sale of art and handicrafts.
✉ Iriarte 24 (off Calle Serrano) and Progreso 4, Santa Cruz

### CASA DE LOS BALCONES
✉ Edificio Olympo, Plaza de la Candelaria, Santa Cruz

### CASA DE LOS CALADOS

✉ Calle Núñez de la Peña 9, La Laguna

### MERCADO DE ARTESANÍA ESPAÑOLA

✉ Plaza de la Candelaria 8, Santa Cruz

## THE WEST

### ARTESANÍA DEL LINO

✉ Calle Santo Domingo, Puerto de la Cruz

### CASA DE LOS BALCONES

This beautifully restored 17th-century mansion (► 16) contains a craft shop where local people can often be seen at work. As well as inexpensive souvenirs, a wide range of high-quality items, such as Spanish and Canarian lace and linen and traditional Canarian embroideries, are on sale. Some are made on the

premises, as the Casa de los Balcones also serves
as a highly regarded school of embroidery.
✉ Calle San Francisco 3, La Orotava

### CASA DE LOS BALCONES
✉ Paseo de San Telmo 22, Puerto de la Cruz

### CASA DEL TURISTA
Located opposite La Orotava's famous Casa de
los Balcones (➤ 205), this craft and souvenir
shop stocks similar products.
✉ Calle San Francisco 4, La Orotava

### CASA IRIARTE
Fine selection of hand-worked table linen.
✉ Calle San Juan 17, Puerto de la Cruz

### CASA TORREHERMOSA (ARTENERIFE)
Run by the state-run crafts organisation and
specialises in genuine local work. There is a craft
museum attached.
✉ Calle Tomás Zerolo 27, La Orotava ☎ 922 334013

## THE SOUTH

### CANARIA OCÉANO

Exhibitions and sale of crafts.

✉ Carretera General de Chío, Guía de Isora

### CASA DE LOS BALCONES

A wide range of inexpensive crafts.

✉ Gran Hotel Bahía del Duque Fañabe, Costa Adeje

### MERCADO DE ARTESANÍA ESPAÑOLA

An interesting stop on the way into the Teide National Park.

✉ Carretera General, Vilaflor

## LA GOMERA

### ARTESANÍA LOS TELARES

See weaving and other local crafts in production before you buy. Similar *artesanía* at Agulo, about 3km away.

✉ Hermigua 🕙 Mon–Sat

### MARKET

Gomeran craftwork and local products at the morning market.

✉ Avenida de Colón, San Sebastián

# BARGAINS/MARKETS

## BARGAINS

As a duty-free region, the Canary Islands are like a big duty-free shop, selling perfumes, cameras, binoculars and other optical goods, CD players and electronic goods, at lower prices than at home (➤ 203).

In the big towns and main resorts, several Asian-run 'Bazaars' are the usual outlet for these goods. Marked prices are generally open to a bit of haggling, though some stores make a point of not negotiating – a selling point with Europeans who dread haggling! Prices are similar to those in airport shops and other duty-free outlets. Before buying, it helps to know what the price is back home and whether the guarantee will be valid. The main outlets are Calle de Castillo, Santa Cruz; Playa de las Américas and Puerto de la Cruz.

## MARKETS AND HAWKERS

Genuine markets like Mercado Nuestra Señora de África in Santa Cruz (➤ 30) are the place to find fresh fruit and vegetables, kitchenware, fabrics and household items.

Most other Tenerife markets attract European hippy 'artists'

and African traders, selling a repetitive range of kitsch, beads and home-made jewellery, and leather goods. Some of them occasionally offer original or interesting items. They are often joined by Spanish stallholders offering either bargain clothes and beachwear, or lace, crochet and embroidery, especially tablecloths, placemats, napkins, bedlinen and handkerchiefs. These are not always offered at low prices, but they represent good value for such high-quality handmade work.You may also find glazed pottery and crockery, attractively hand-painted. When not at the markets, the hippies and African traders often hawk their goods in streets and on the beaches.

## MAIN MARKETS

### LOS ABRIGOS
NIGHT MARKET
🕓 Tue 6–10

### LOS CRISTIANOS
✉ Next to Hotel Arona Gran 🕓 Sun 9–2

### PLAYA DE LAS AMÉRICAS
✉ Torviscas 🕓 Thu, Sat 9–2

## PUERTO DE LA CRUZ
### MERCADO MUNICIPAL SAN FELIPE
✉ Avenida de Blas Pérez Gonzáles ⏱ Mon–Sat am

## SANTA CRUZ
### MERCADO NUESTRA SEÑORA DE ÁFRICA
✉ Just off Calle de San Sebastián ⏱ Mon–Sat 8–1

### RASTRO (FLEA MARKET)
✉ Near the *mercado*, Calle José Manuel Guimerá ⏱ Sun 10–2

## SAN SEBASTIÁN, LA GOMERA
✉ Avenida de Colón ⏱ Mon–Sat am

## TACORONTE
### FARMERS' MARKET
⏱ Sat pm, Sun am

# ARTS, DRAMA & EXCURSIONS

## ARTS AND DRAMA

Tenerife has several art galleries, museums, concert halls and theatres. Most of the island's culture is firmly located in the north, well away from the tourist sites.

### LA LAGUNA

The town of La Laguna, little frequented by tourists, is Tenerife's centre of contemporary culture. Each year it hosts the island's Jazz Festival and International Theatre Festival.

### TEATRO LEAL

A former theatre and arts centre used to host concerts, exhibitions and festival events – due to be closed for restoration during 2005.

✉ Calle Obispo Rey Redondo

### SANTA CRUZ
#### AUDITORIO DE TENERIFE

Tenerife's excellent concert hall for opera and classical music, designed by Spanish architect Santiago Calatrava Valls, is the home of the Orquesta Symphony Orchestra of Tenerife. Entertainment staged here includes *zarzuela* (Spanish light opera) and musicals, as well as jazz, rock and world music. The Auditorio de Tenerife is the venue for the island's annual Music Festival, the archipelago's leading classical music event (begins early January for 3 to 4 weeks).

✉ Calle Cruz Verde 21–23 ☎ 922 270611

### TEATRO GUIMERÁ

Plays (Spanish-language only), opera and concerts – and home of the first-class Symphony Orchestra of Tenerife, which gives performances all year.

✉ Plaza Isla de la Madera ☎ 922 606265

## BOAT EXCURSIONS

Many tour operators and local travel firms organise boat excursions from Costa Adeje, Los Cristianos, Playa de las Américas and Costa del Silencio. Day trips to La Gomera are especially popular. Other boat trips have no goal except fun, such as the many *sangría* excursions and pirate adventures, which include lunch and usually a swimming stop.

## WHALE-WATCHING

About 200 pilot whales live in the Canary Island waters, usually on the south side of the archipelago. A good place to spot whales is between Los Cristianos and Los Gigantes; dolphins can also be found. Boat trips to see them are a highlight for visitors.

### NOSTRAMO
Successful and popular boat excursions in a beautiful Spanish schooner built in 1918. As well as seeing dolphins and whales, there is an unforgettable lunch stop below the Los Gigantes cliffs and a pause in Masca Bay for a chance to swim.

✉ Playa San Juan, Playa de las Américas ☎ 922 750085 (Playa de las Américas), 922 385116 (Puerto de la Cruz) 🕓 Departs daily 10am
🚌 Free bus from southern resorts

### TROPICAL DELFIN
Modern excursion boat with underwater windows to view the sea life.

✉ South Pier, Puerto Colón, Playa de las Américas ☎ 922 750149
🕓 Daily trips 10.30, 1.30

# SPORT

## GOLF

Many visitors come to Tenerife just to play on the excellent golf courses, four of which are in the area between Playa de las Américas and Reina Sofía Airport.

If you are playing and staying in the south, visit the northern golf course at least once – for the amazing contrast of lush greenery. Each of the golf courses has formed partnerships with nearby hotels, whose resident guests enjoy reduced green fees (enquire at the clubs for details).

### NORTH

### EL PEÑON CLUB DE GOLF TENERIFE

An 18-hole course founded in 1932 by British expatriates.

✉ Tacoronte, 2km from Los Rodeos Airport, 14km from Santa Cruz ☎ 922 636607

### GOLF LA ROSALEDA

Puerto's golf course and school is laid out amid a lush setting of banana plantations and other trees, with views to the Orotava Valley and Mont Teide. Apart from the par-3 nine-hole course, there is a driving range, putting green and a cafeteria.

✉ Camino Carrasco 13, Puerto de la Cruz ☎ 922 373000

## SOUTH

### AMARILLA GOLF

An 18-hole course beside coastal cliffs.

✉ Urbanización Amarilla Golf, San Miguel de Abona ☎ 922 730319

### GOLF DEL SUR

This 27-hole course has hosted several major international events.

✉ Urbanización Golf del Sur, San Miguel de Abona ☎ 922 738170

### COSTA ADEJE GOLF

This fine 27-hole course has greens with several doglegs. Located 5km from Playa de las Américas, with views of La Gomera.

✉ Finca de los Olivos, Adeje ☎ 922 710000

### GOLF LAS AMÉRICAS

A 72-par course just outside Playa de las Américas and Los Cristianos; 18 holes.

✉ Exit 28 of Autopista del Sur ☎ 922 752005

### CENTRO DE GOLF LOS PALOS

A par-27 nine-hole course, just 6km east of Playa de las Américas. Small but plenty of challenges.

✉ Carretera Guaza–Las Galletas km 7, Arona ☎ 922 169080

## WATERSPORTS

Scuba and offshore diving is popular all around the islands. Several centres offer a good standard and are staffed by qualified instructors. Diving courses should meet PADI standards and also check insurance cover.

Near-constant trade winds and warm unpolluted waters ensure ideal conditions for windsurfing and surfing around the island's south coast. One of the best locations is

El Médano beach, close to Reina Sofía Airport. Waters on the north coast are too rough for safe surfing.

### BARLOVENTO
Canoeing, sailing, water-skiing, windsurfing and boat rental.
✉ Parque Marítino César Manrique, Santa Cruz ☎ 922 223840

### CENTRO DE BUCEO ATLANTIK
✉ Hotel Maritim, Calle El Burgado 1, Puerto de la Cruz
☎ 922 362801

### CENTRO INSULAR DE DEPORTES MARINOS (CIDEMAT)
Canoeing, diving, sailing, water-skiing and windsurfing.
✉ Carretera Santa Cruz–San Andrés ☎ 922 240945

## SPA

### AQUA CLUB THERMAL
This upmarket Costa Adeje leisure complex has a huge swimming pool, fountains, a seawater pool, sauna, Turkish bath and many more high quality spa and fitness facilities.
✉ Calle Galicia, Torviscas Alto, Adeje ☎ 922 716555

## GO-KARTING

**KARTING CLUB TENERIFE**
This club has one of the best kart circuits in Europe.
✉ Carretera de Cho, at km 66, off the southern Autopista at Guaza
☎ 922 786620

## WALKING, CLIMBING, CYCLING

Graded footpaths marked and maintained by ICONA, the Spanish conservation agency, criss-cross the island. The agency issues a number of maps (available in tourist offices and park visitor centres on the island) showing marked walks. These include a pocket-size pack of 22 different footpath maps, with

descriptions in English and some history about each area and the landmarks, flora and fauna. Discovery Walking Guides and Sunflower Guides (available in the UK) are useful additions aimed at the walker.

### ADEN TENERIFE MULTIAVENTURA

This highly proficient multi-adventure sports centre organises cycling tours, mountain cycling, horse riding, walking excursions and climbing.

✉ Calle Castillo (Oficina 307) 41, Santa Cruz ☎ 922 246261

## WRESTLING

One of the traditional island sports, called *la lucha* or *lucha canaria*, descended from pre-Spanish (Guanche times), is a curious form of wrestling. With its own weekly TV show and frequent matches – which send the usually restrained Canarios wild with excitement – Canarian wrestling has become very popular in recent years. Two teams compete by pitting one man against another, in turns, until there is a clear victory. The men, wearing a particular style of shorts and shirt, try to throw each other to the ground by gripping the side of each other's clothing. It is slow and careful, with sudden moves as the men try to catch each other off guard. Tourists are welcome to watch matches; ask at hotels or the tourist office for match details and venues. Demonstrations of *lucha canaria* are given at the Hotel Tigaiga:

✉ Parque Taoro 28, Puerto de la Cruz ☎ 922 383500 ⊕ Sun 11am

# NIGHTLIFE

## CASINOS

### CASINO PLAYA DE LAS AMÉRICAS

Place your bets at the Hotel Gran Tinerfe.

✉ Avenida Rafael Puig Llurina, Playa de las Américas ☎ 922 794903
🕐 From 7pm

### CASINO SANTA CRUZ

Dress up for an evening of roulette, blackjack and poker at Tenerife's poshest hotel.

✉ Hotel Mencey, Avenida Doctor José Naveiras 38, Santa Cruz
☎ 922 574324 🕐 From 8pm

### CASINO TAORO

Tenerife's grandest casino. Cocktails, restaurant, slot machines, roulette and gambling tables. Casual dressers are not admitted, there's a modest entrance charge, and you must take your passport.

✉ Parque Taoro, Puerto de la Cruz ☎ 922 383742 🕐 From 8pm

# PUBS, CLUBS AND DISCOS

## LOS CRISTIANOS/PLAYA DE LAS AMÉRICAS

Las Veronicas, on the seafront road in Playa de las Américas is the focal point for entertainment. Things liven up around 11pm, bars close 3am–6am.

### BOBBY'S

Rated one of Playa's top dance clubs; gets going very late.

✉ Centro Comercial Veronicas, Playa de las Americas

### BUSBY'S

Right next door to Bobby's and sharing the same crowd.

✉ Centro Comercial Veronicas, Playa de las Americas

### CALEDONIAN BAR (THE CALLY)

Terrific young atmosphere and music at this disco pub.

✉ Centro Comercial Starco, Playa de las Américas

### LINEKERS BAR

Booze, telly, bar food and music and dance prevails at this noisy popular laddish sports pub opposite Las Veronicas.

✉ Centro Comercial Starco, Playa de las Américas

### PRISMAS
✉ Hotel Tenerife Sol, Playa de las Américas ☎ 922 790371

### TRAMPS
Very, very popular disco – but periodically closed.
✉ Centro Comercial Veronicas, Playa de las Americas ☎ 922 790371

## PUERTO DE LA CRUZ
Quieter, slightly older holiday crowds frequent these venues.

### BLUE NOTE
A well-known jazz spot.
✉ Calle Zamora 15

### QATAR
✉ Calle Aceviño, Urbanización La Paz

### CONCORDIA CLUB
✉ Avenida de Venezuela 3

### JOY
✉ Obispo Pérez Cáceres

### VAMPI'S
✉ Edif. Drago – Bajo, Avenida Generalisimo

### VICTORIA
✉ Hotel Tenerife Playa, Avenida de Colón

## SANTA CRUZ
The clientele who jam into Santa Cruz's nightspots are mainly young Spanish visitors, and the more adventurous among the foreign tourists.

### DAIDA
✉ Calle Carlos Hamilton, Residencial Anaga

### KU
✉ Parque la Granja

### NOOCTUA
✉ Avenida Anaga 37

# DINNER DANCE, NIGHTCLUBS AND CABARET

Known here as 'show restaurants', many places offer floorshows and entertainment while the audience is dining or drinking. Some are very slick, featuring international entertainers. Others offer a more risqué type of performance, with showgirls dressed in feathers and not much else.

## PUERTO DE LA CRUZ AND THE WEST
### ANDROMEDA

This popular, stylish cabaret and show restaurant was created by artist César Manrique and is located at the Lago Martiánez on the seafront. It attracts world-class artistes and highly professional dancers and showgirls.

✉ Isla del Lago, Lago Martiánez, Puerto de la Cruz ☎ 922 383852

🕐 Dinner 8pm, floor show 10pm

### BARBACOA TACORANTE

Folklore show based on Tenerife's carnival. Colourful costumes and a barbecue-style dinner.

✉ Calle Garoé, Urbanización La Paz, Peurto de la Cruz

☎ 922 382910

### TENERIFE PALACE
Start the evening with a complimentary cocktail. Show starts at 10pm.
✉ Camino del Coche, Puerto de la Cruz
☎ 922 382960

## PLAYA DE LAS AMÉRICAS AND THE SOUTH
### LA BALLENA
A show-restaurant in Ten-Bel, on the Costa del Silencio.
✉ Ten-Bel ☎ 922 730060

### PIRÁMIDES DE ARONA
Ambitious gala performances featuring cabaret, opera, ballet and flamenco.
✉ Mare Nostrum Resort, Avenida de las Américas, Playa de las Américas ☎ 922 757549

### TABLAO FLAMENCO
See flamenco shows while you dine.
✉ Avenida Rafael Puig Lluvina, Playa de las Américas ☎ 922 797611

# WHAT'S ON WHEN

## JANUARY

*Cabalgata de los Reyes Magos* (The Three Kings Cavalcade, 5–6 Jan): many places, especially Santa Cruz and Valle Gran Rey (La Gomera)

*Fiestas* (17–22 Jan): Garachico, Icod de los Vinos, Los Realejos and San Sebastián (La Gomera)

## FEBRUARY

The whole month is called Carnival Month, with a festive mood everywhere.

*Candelaria* (Candlemas, 2 Feb): big festival and pilgrimage in certain towns and villages, especially Candelaria

*Carnaval* (one week around 8–15 Feb): Santa Cruz and Puerto de la Cruz – huge events, parades, festivities. The climax is Shrove Tuesday, the biggest event of the year.

*Carnaval* (end Feb): Los Cristianos – marks the end of Tenerife's Carnival Month

*Carnaval* (end Feb/early Mar): San Sebastián (La Gomera)

## MARCH/APRIL

*San José holiday* (19 Mar)

*Semana Santa* (Holy Week): big events, often sober in character, all over the islands during Easter Week
*Fiestas* (25 Apr): especially at Icod de los Vinos, Teguesta and Agulo (La Gomera)

## MAY/JUNE
*Día de las Islas Canarias* (Canary Islands Day, 30 May): throughout the archipelago
*Corpus Christi* (late May/early Jun): Octavo (8 days) of huge celebrations throughout the island, especially La Orotava, La Laguna and Vilaflor. Streets are decorated with sand and flower designs.
*Romería* (after Corpus Christi): the season of local pilgrimages
*Fiesta de San Juan* (24 Jun): midsummer celebrated at Vallehermoso (La Gomera) and other villages

## JULY
*Fiestas del Gran Poder* (15 Jul): Puerto de la Cruz – processions, parades, fireworks and fun
*Santiago* (25 Jul): festive public holiday; Santa Cruz, celebration of the defeat of Rear Admiral Nelson (1797)

## AUGUST

*Asunción and Nuestra Señora de la Candelaria* (15 Aug):
Candelaria – important pilgrimage festival involving the whole
of Tenerife
*Romería de San Roque* (16 Aug): Garachico – popular,
colourful local event
*Nuestra Señora del Carmen* (30 Aug): Los Cristianos – lively
fiesta

## SEPTEMBER

*Semana Colombina* (Columbus Week, 1–6 Sep): San
Sebastián (La Gomera)
*Virgen de Buen* Paso (15 Sep): Alajeró (La Gomera)
*Fiestas* (mid-Sep): La Laguna and Tacoronte

## OCTOBER

*Día de la Hispanidad* (12 Oct): celebrating Columbus
*Fiesta de los Cacharros* (Pots and Pans, 29 Oct): noisy fiesta
to celebrate the arrival of the new wine

## NOVEMBER/DECEMBER

*Holidays* (1 Nov, 6 Dec, 8 Dec, 25 Dec)

What you
need to know

# Language guide

People working in the tourist industry, including waiters, generally know some English. In places where few tourists venture, including bars and restaurants in Santa Cruz, it is helpful to know some basic Spanish.

Pronunciation guide: *b* almost like a *v*; *c* before *e* or *i* sounds like *th* otherwise like *k*; *d* can be like English *d* or like a *th*; *g* before *e* or *i* is a guttural *h*, between vowels like *h*, otherwise like *g*; *h* always silent; *j* guttural *h*; *ll* like English *lli* (as in 'million'); *ñ* sounds like *ni* in 'onion'; *qu* sound like *k*; *v* sounds a little like *b*; *z* like English *th*.

| | | | |
|---|---|---|---|
| hotel | **hotel** | breakfast | **el desayuno** |
| room | **una habitación** | bathroom | **el cuarto de baño** |
| single/double/twin | **individual/doble/con dos camas** | shower | **la ducha** |
| | | balcony | **el balcón** |
| one/two nights | **una noche / dos noches** | reception | **la recepción** |
| reservation | **una reserva** | key | **la llave** |
| rate | **la tarifa** | room service | **el servicio de habitaciones** |

| | | | |
|---|---|---|---|
| bureau de change | **cambio** | US dollars | **dólares** |
| post office | **correos** | banknote | **un billete de** |
| cash machine/ATM | **cajero automático** | | **banco** |
| foreign exchange | **cambio (de** | traveller's cheques | **cheques de viaje** |
| | **divisas)** | credit card | **la tarjeta de** |
| foreign currency | **cambio** | | **crédito** |
| pounds sterling | **libras esterlinas** | | |

| | | | |
|---|---|---|---|
| restaurant | **restaurante** | dessert | **el postre** |
| cafe-bar | **bar** | water | **agua** |
| table | **una mesa** | (house) wine | **vino (de la casa)** |
| menu | **la carta** | beer | **cerveza** |
| set main course | **plato combinado** | drink | **la bebida** |
| today's set menu | **el plato del día** | bill | **la cuenta** |
| wine list | **la carta de vinos** | toilets | **los servicios** |
| cheers! | **salud!** | | |

| | | | | |
|---|---|---|---|---|
| plane | **el avion** | | ticket office | **el despacho de billetes** |
| airport | **el aeropuerto** | | timetable | **el horario** |
| bus | **el guagua/autobús** | | seat | **un asiento** |
| ferry | **el ferry** | | reserved seat | **un asiento reservado** |
| terminal | **terminus** | | | |
| ticket | **un billete** | | | |
| single/return… | **una ida/de ida y vuelta…** | | | |

| | | | | |
|---|---|---|---|---|
| yes | **si** | | Is there…? | **Hay…?** |
| no | **no** | | Do you have …? | |
| please | **por favor** | | I don't speak Spanish | **No hablo español** |
| thank you | **gracias** | | I am… | **Soy…** |
| Hello/hi | **Hola!** | | I have… | **Tengo…** |
| Hello/good day | **Buenos dias** | | Help! | **Socorro!** |
| Sorry, pardon me | **Perdon** | | How much? | **Cuánto es?** |
| Bye, see you | **Hasta luego** | | open | **abierto** |
| that's fine | **está bien** | | closed | **cerrado** |
| What? | **Como?** | | | |

# Practicalities

## WHAT YOU NEED

- ● Required
- ○ Suggested
- ▲ Not required

Some countries require a passport to remain valid for a minimum period (usually at least six months) beyond the date of entry – contact their consulate or embassy or your travel agent for details.

| | UK | Germany | USA | Netherlands | Spain |
|---|---|---|---|---|---|
| Passport/National Identity Card | ● | ● | ● | ● | ● |
| Visa (regulations can change – check before your journey) | ▲ | ▲ | ▲ | ▲ | ▲ |
| Onward or Return Ticket | ▲ | ▲ | ● | ▲ | ▲ |
| Health Inoculations | ▲ | ▲ | ▲ | ▲ | ▲ |
| Health Documentation (reciprocal agreement document, ➤ 248, Health) | ▲ | ▲ | ▲ | ▲ | ▲ |
| Travel Insurance | ○ | ○ | ○ | ○ | ○ |
| Driving Licence (national – EU format/national/Spanish trnsltn/interntnal) | ● | ● | ● | ● | ● |
| Car Insurance Certificate (if own car) | ● | ● | ● | ● | ● |
| Car Registration Document (if own car) | ● | ● | ● | ● | ● |

## TOURIST OFFICES

### In the UK

Spanish National Tourist Office
22–23 Manchester Square
London W1M 5AP
☎ 020 7486 8077
www.tourspain.co.uk

### In the USA

Tourist Office of Spain
666 Fifth Avenue, 35th floor
New York, NY 10103
☎ 212 265-8822
www.okspain.org/

Other TOs in Chicago, Los Angeles, Miami.

## CUSTOMS

### YES

There are no restrictions at all on goods taken into Tenerife or other Canary Islands.

It would be pointless to take most goods into these islands in the expectation of saving money, however, as almost everything is cheaper in the Canaries than it is at home. If you are carrying a large amount of money, you should declare it on arrival to avoid explanations on departure.

### NO

There are a few obvious exceptions to the information on ths page, notably illegal drugs, firearms, obscene material and unlicensed animals.

## WHEN TO GO

### Average temperatures for Tenerife

|  |  |  |  | High season |  |  |  |  |  |  |  |
|---|---|---|---|---|---|---|---|---|---|---|---|
|  |  |  |  | Low season |  |  |  |  |  |  |  |

| 20°C | 21°C | 23°C | 24°C | 25°C | 27°C | 28°C | 29°C | 28°C | 26°C | 23°C | 20°C |
|---|---|---|---|---|---|---|---|---|---|---|---|
| JAN | FEB | MAR | APR | MAY | JUN | JUL | AUG | SEP | OCT | NOV | DEC |

Very wet    Wet    Cloud    Sun    Sunshine & showers

## ARRIVING

**By Air** Most flights to Tenerife arrive at Reina Sofía (or Tenerife Sur) Airport (☎ 922 759200), on the Costa del Silencio near Playa de las Américas in the south. A second airport, Los Rodeos or Tenerife Norte (☎ 922 6359880), at La Laguna in the north, is mainly used for domestic flights. There are daily flights from Tenerife Norte airport to La Gomera.

**By Sea** Independent travellers can reach the islands on a slow boat from Cadiz, on the Spanish mainland. Inter-island ferries and hydrofoils connect Tenerife and La Gomera to the other islands.

**Reina Sofía Airport to:**

Puerto de la Cruz: 100km

Playa de las Americas: 15km

**Journey times**

N/A

30 minutes

10 minutes

## MONEY

The euro is the single currency of the European Monetary Union, which has been adopted by 12 member states including Spain.. There are banknotes for 5, 10, 20, 50, 100, 200 and 500 euros, and coins for 1, 2, 5, 10, 20 and 50 cents, and 1 and 2 euros. ATMs (cash machines) can be found in major towns and resorts. Euro traveller's cheques are widely accepted.

€10                    €50                    €100                    €200

## TIME

The time in Tenerife (and all the Canary Islands) is the same as in the UK. Sometimes a temporary 1-hour time difference occurs when clocks go forward or back in March and September. The Canary Islands are 5 hours ahead of the eastern US.

## TOURIST OFFICES

**Tenerife**

*Airport Tenerife Sur Reina Sofia*
☎ 922 392037

*Los Cristianos*
CC Casa de la Cultura, Calle General Franco
☎ 922 757137

*Playa de las Américas*
Centro Comercial City Centre
☎ 922 797668

*Puerto de la Cruz*
Plaza de Europa 5
☎ 922 386000

*Santa Cruz*
Palacio Insular (ground floor), Plaza de España
☎ 922 239592

**La Gomera**

*Playa de Santiago*
Edificio Las Vistas, Local 8, Avenida Marítima
☎ 922 895650

*San Sebastián*
Calle Real 4
☎ 922 141512

**Websites**
Spanish National Tourist Office:
www.spain.info

**Local information:**
www.cabtfe.es/puntoinfo
www.puntoinfo.idecnet.com

## NATIONAL HOLIDAYS

| JAN | FEB | MAR | APR | MAY | JUN | JUL | AUG | SEP | OCT | NOV | DEC |
|-----|-----|-----|-----|-----|-----|-----|-----|-----|-----|-----|-----|
| 2 | 1 | (2) | (1) | 2 | 1 | 1 | 1 | 0 | 1 | 1 | 3 |

| | | | | |
|---|---|---|---|---|
| 1 Jan | Año Nuevo (New Year's Day) | | 25 Jul | Santiago (St James' Day) |
| 6 Jan | Los Reyes (Epiphany) | | 15 Aug | Asunción (Assumption) |
| 2 Feb | La Candelaria (Candlemas) | | 12 Oct | Hispanidad (Columbus Day) |
| 19 Mar | San José (St Joseph's Day) | | 1 Nov | Todos los Santos (All Saints' Day) |
| Mar/Apr | Pascua (Easter) Thu, Fri, Sun of | | 6 Dec | Constitución (Constitution Day) |
| | Easter Week, and following Mon | | 8 Dec | Immaculada Concepción |
| 1 May | Dia del Trabajo (Labour Day) | | | (Immaculate Conception) |
| May/Jun | Corpus Christi | | 25 Dec | Navidad (Christmas Day) |

## OPENING HOURS

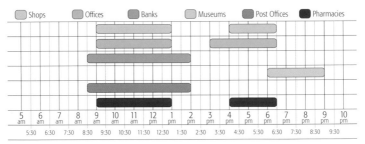

**Shops**: most shops are open Mon–Sat 9–1, 4–8.

**Offices**: usually Mon–Fri 9–1, 3–7.

**Banks**: Mon–Fri 8:30–2, Sat 9–1 (closed Sat 1 Jun–31 Oct).

**Museums**: 4–7pm; larger sites open mornings too.

**Post Offices**: Mon–Fri 8:30–2, Sat 9–1.

**Pharmacies**: as shops but closed Sat afternoons. Normally at least one open after hours (rota on door).

## PERSONAL SAFETY

Street crime is quite rare in Tenerife and
La Gomera but visitors should not be
complacent. Uniformed police are always
present in tourist areas. The greatest risk is
assault or theft by another tourist.

Lock doors and windows before going out.

Put all valuables in the boot of your car.

Fire is a risk in hotels – locate the nearest
fire exit to your room and ensure it is not
blocked or locked.

Do not leave possessions unattended on the
beach or in cars.

**Police assistance:**
☎ 112 or 091

## PUBLIC TRANSPORT

**Buses** are always called by their local name, *guaguas* (pronounced wah-wahs). The stops are called *paradas* and are indicated by a letter P. A bus station is called an *estación de guaguas*. Most Tenerife buses are operated by TITSA. Services are fairly frequent and inexpensive on main routes between towns. Off the main roads, and throughout La Gomera, service is intermittent and generally of little use to visitors. If you plan to use buses a lot, save up to 50 per cent by purchasing a multi-trip TITSA Bono-Bus card. TITSA hotline (English language) ☎ 922 531300.

**Main bus stations** Avenida Béthencourt, Playa de las Américas ☎ 922 795427

Avenida 3 Mayo 47, Santa Cruz ☎ 922 218122

Calle de Cupido, Puerto de la Cruz ☎ 922 381807

La Laguna ☎ 922 259412

Many of the main attractions operate free shuttle buses to and from the resorts.

**Ferries** Transmediterránea (Est. Marítima, Muelle de Ribera, Santa Cruz ☎ 922 842244): to mainland Spain and other Canary Islands from Santa Cruz; from Los Cristianos (Muelle de Los Cristianos) to La Gomera (Estacíon Marítima, Puerto de San Sebastían de la Gomera ☎ 922 871324). Estación Jet-Foil (Muelle Norte, Santa Cruz ☎ 922 243012): 80-minute jetfoil to Las Palmas de Gran Canaria.Estación Hidro-Foil (Los Cristianos harbour ☎ 922 796178): hydrofoils to La Gomera (35 mins). Ferry Gomera (Los Cristianos harbour ☎ 922 790215): to La Gomera (90 mins).

Fred Olsen (Muelle Ribera, Santa Cruz ☎ 922 628200): to La Gomera and Gran Canaria from Los Christianos and Santa Cruz.

## DRIVING

Speed limit on motorways: **100–120kph**
Speed limit on other main roads: **100kph**
Speed limit in towns: **40kph**

Seat belts are compulsory for all passengers. Children under 10 (excluding babies in rear-facing baby seats) must ride in the back seats. If you need child seats, it is strongly advised to book ahead.

Driving under the influence of alcohol is strictly illegal and random breath tests are carried out; the consequences of being involved in an accident could result in a jail term.

Unleaded petrol (*sin plomo*) is the norm. Petrol stations on main roads are usually open 24hrs and most take credit cards. Off main roads they may be far apart, closed on Sunday, and don't always take credit cards.

Rented cars and their drivers should all be insured by the rental company. In the event of a breakdown, call the car rental company's emergency number.

Hefty on-the-spot fines are levied for not wearing seat belts, not stopping at a Stop sign or overtaking where forbidden.

## CAR RENTAL

It is relatively inexpensive to rent a car on Tenerife, but pricier on La Gomera. The small local car firms are efficient (ask for an after-hours emergency number), though the international firms are represented. Drivers must be over 21. A good road map is essential.

## TELEPHONES

To call the operator, dial 1009. To use a phone in a bar, simply pay the charge requested at the end of the call – the barman has a meter to check the cost. To use a public pay phone, you'll usually need *una tarjeta de telefóno*, a phone card – available from tobacconists and similar shops. There are also useful phone offices marked *telefónica internacional* where you pay a clerk after the call.

**International Dialling Codes**
From Tenerife to:

| | |
|---|---|
| UK: 00 44 | Ireland: 00 353 |
| USA: 00 1 | Spain: dial number only |

## POST

### Post Offices

Postboxes are yellow and often have a slot marked *Extranjeros* for mail to foreign countries. Letters and postcards to the UK: 50c (up to 20gms). Air letters and postcards to the US/Canada: 75c (up to 15gms). Letters within Spain: 20c. Buy stamps at tobacconists, souvenir shops or post offices (*correos y telegrafos*).

## TIPS/GRATUITIES

Yes ✓    No ✗

| | | |
|---|---|---|
| Hotels & Restaurants | ✗ | Included |
| Room Service | ✓ | €1-2 |
| Cafés/bars | ✓ | change |
| Taxis | ✓ | 10% |
| Porters | ✓ | €1-2 |
| Chambermaids | ✓ | €1-2 |
| Ushers/usherettes at shows & events | ✓ | change |
| Hairdressers (women's) | ✓ | €2-3 |
| Cloakroom/washroom attendants | ✓ | 50c |
| Tour guide | ✓ | €2-3 |

## HEALTH

**Insurance** It is essential to have good medical health cover in case of a medical emergency. Hospital doctors within the state scheme will accept Form E111 from UK residents for free emergency treatment, but the process of reimbursement is complicated and bureaucratic. You may need to give a photocopy of Form E111 to the doctor. To claim on medical insurance you may need to show that you did request treatment under the E111 scheme.

**Dental Services** Emergency treatment can be expensive but is covered by most medical insurance (but not by Form E111). Hotel receptionists and holiday reps can generally advise on a local dentist.

**Sun Advice** The biggest danger to health here is too much sun. Remember that the Canaries are 700 miles nearer the Equator than southern Spain and on the same latitude as the Sahara. Use generous amounts of sun cream with a high protection factor. A wide-brimmed hat and a T-shirt (even when swimming) are advisable for children.

**Medication** Any essential prescribed medications should be taken with you to Tenerife or La Gomera. Well-known over-the-counter proprietary brands of analgesics and popular remedies are available at all pharmacies. All medicines must be paid for, even if prescribed by a doctor.

**Safe Water** Tap water is safe all over the islands, except where signs indicate otherwise. The taste may be slightly salty. Bottled water is recommended.

## HOSPITALS AND CLINICS

**Santa Cruz**
University Hospital ☎ 922 790401
Candelaria Hospital ☎ 922 766362
Rambla Hospital ☎ 922 790505

**Puerto de la Cruz and the North**
Bellevue clinic ☎ 922 791417
Tamaragua clinic ☎ 922 380512

The Medical Centre (24/7 English speaking)
☎ 900 100090

**Playa de las Américas and the South**
Las Americas ☎ 922 750022
Clinica San Eugenio ☎ 922 791000
International Mediservice ☎ 922 790563

## ELECTRICITY

The voltage is 220–225v. Sockets take the standard European two-round-pin plugs. Bring an adaptor for any British or American appliances you wish to use with their usual plugs, and Americans should change the voltage setting on appliances, or bring a voltage transformer.

## TAXIS

Cabs display a special SP licence plate (*servicio público*). Some taxi ranks display fares between principal destinations. In addition, taxi drivers offer island tours for up to four passengers; negotiate the fare before you set off.

# Index

# Index

## ACKNOWLEDGEMENTS

The Automobile Association wishes to thank the following photo libraries for their assistance in the preparation of this book.

**Corbis** UK 215; **Digitalvision** 225; **Photodisc** 218, 238.

The remaining photographs are held in the Association's own photo library (AA World Travel Library) and were taken by the following photographers:

**Caroline Jones** 2tl, 2c, 2/3, 19, 20, 22, 24, 32, 36, 48, 54, 57, 57b/g, 60, 67, 68 71, 77, 81, 82, 101, 108, 126, 147, 164, 175, 180/1, 187, 190, 220, 222, 228, 247; **Max Jourdan** 227; **Rob Moore** 2bl, 14/5, 16, 21, 35, 45, 74, 109, 111, 125, 130, 145, 148, 156, 159, 168/9, 196/7, 199, 202, 212, 231, 254/5; **Ken Paterson** 211; **Clive Sawyer** front cover, 1, 2tr, 10/1, 25, 26, 27, 29, 31, 38/9, 69, 76, 79, 89, 90/1, 94, 95, 97, 98, 100, 103, 104, 106, 112, 114, 116, 118, 123, 129, 133, 134, 138/9, 142, 146, 153, 163, 167, 170/1, 177, 178, 182, 1? 188, 189, 192, 195, 201, 206, 246; **James Tims** 3br, 13, 33, 47, 50, 53, 55, 58/9, 62, 64/5, 66, 72, 85, 86, 115, 119, 120/1, 122, 137, 150, 151, 154, 2 209, 217, 232/3, 243.

Typesetting: **Information Engineers**  Page layout: **Pentacor book design**
Editors: **Marilynne Lanng**, **Pam Stagg**  Design support: **Katherine Mead**